KT-522-430

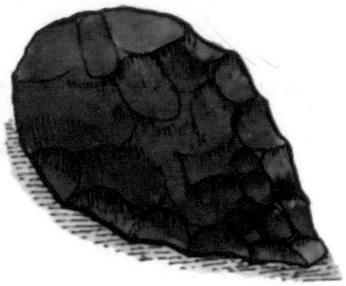

53½ THINGS

THAT·CHANGED·THE·WORLD

AND · SOME · THAT · DIDN'T!

By
DAVID WEST

Written by
STEVE PARKER

BOOK HOUSE

D 00 0011069

THE 53½ THINGS

BEFORE HISTORY BEGAN 6
WALKING ON TWO LEGS • TOOLS • FIRE • CLOTHES • ART • MUSIC • WORSHIP • TOWNS • FARMING • WINES AND BEERS • HORSE-RIDING • WHEELS • BRONZE AND IRON • ARMIES • BOATS • POTTERY • GLASS • THE RULE OF THE LAW • SCHOOLS • VOTES FOR THE PEOPLE

THE TOILET 12
THE BLAST FURNACE 14
THE ROAD 15
THE CLOCK 16
THE PIANO 17
THE PLOUGH 18
THE COMBINE HARVESTER 19
THE SAIL 20
THE SCREW 21
THE TELESCOPE AND MICROSCOPE 22
THE PRINTING PRESS 24
MEDICINE 26
THE ELECTRIC LIGHT 28
THE ELECTRIC MOTOR 29
THE PHONOGRAPH 30
GUNS AND GUNPOWDER 32
TELEPHONES AND MOBILES 34
RADIO 36
TELEVISION 37
THE STEAM ENGINE 38
THE INTERNAL COMBUSTION ENGINE 40
THE AEROPLANE 42
THE JET ENGINE 44
THE SPACE ROCKET 46
THE SATELLITE 48
THE MAP 50
THE CAMERA 51
OIL 52
ELECTRONICS, COMPUTERS AND THE INTERNET 54
THE ATOMIC BOMB 56
FUSION POWER – *HALF AN INVENTION?* 57

...AND THINGS THAT DIDN'T 58
THE SAFETY PIN • THE RATTLE • TAME CATS • KITES • NAPKINS • CHESS • NATIONAL ANTHEMS • THE UMBRELLA • THE SANDWICH • THE ROCKING CHAIR • INVISIBLE INK • CHEWING GUM • CORNFLAKES • HORSE-RACING ON STAGE • THE TEDDY BEAR • ELECTRIC-ARC IRON • SPRUCE GOOSE • THE MACKEREL CAR • THE MINI-SKIRT • AND FINALLY ... ELECTRIC TRANSPORT?

INDEX 62

SALARIYA

This edition published in MMXII by Book House, an imprint of **The Salariya Book Company Ltd,** 25 Marlborough Place, Brighton, BN1 1UB
www.salariya.com
www.book-house.co.uk

HB ISBN 978-1-908177-53-7
PB ISBN 978-1-908177-54-4

PAPER FROM SUSTAINABLE FORESTS

For Alan, Martin, Jamie and Oliver

Visit our website at **www.book-house.co.uk**
or go to **www.salariya.com** for **free** electronic versions of:
You Wouldn't Want to be an Egyptian Mummy!
You Wouldn't Want to be a Roman Gladiator!
You Wouldn't Want to be a Polar Explorer!
You Wouldn't Want to sail on a 19th-Century Whaling Ship!

1 3 5 7 9 8 6 4 2

A CIP Catalogue record for this book is available from the British Library.

Printed and bound in China.

This book is sold subject to the conditions that it shall not, by way of trade or otherwise, be lent, resold, hired out, or otherwise circulated without the publisher's prior consent in any form or binding or cover other than that in which it is published and without similar condition being imposed on the subsequent purchaser.

Text copyright © MMXII Steve Parker
Illustrations copyright © MMXII David West
All rights reserved. No part of this book may be reproduced, stored in a retrieval system or transmitted in any form or by any means, electronic, mechanical, photocopying, recording or otherwise, without the written permission of the copyright owner.

INTRODUCTION

Long, long ago (in fact, around 4,753.5 million years ago), an immense cloud of gas and dust whirled through space. Slowly the gas and dust came together into a huge ball that was the Earth. It was so hot that rocks melted and volcanoes threw masses of red-hot lava into the poisonous air.

Since its very beginning, the world has been changing. Life began some 3,500 million years ago. The first true fish swam about 500 million years ago. Early dinosaurs roamed the land 230 million years ago. And over two million years ago, another new type of creature appeared. It was the first human, *Homo habilis* or 'Handy Man'.

Using his clever hands and his extra brain power, Handy Man decided that he wasn't going to be pushed around by the world. He was going to change the world instead.

We are still changing the world today. The changes are happening faster and faster. It has truly become our world, full of our buildings, gadgets and machines. Since fashioning the first rock tools of the Stone Age, over two million years ago, we have been inventing things to make life easier, healthier, more comfortable, and more fun.

This book tells you about the 53½ discoveries and inventions that changed the world. Many are so important that, if they had not happened, we could not live our lives as we do now.

Remember them all!

BEFORE HISTORY BEGAN

When written history began, over 5,000 years ago, people could record events and learn from the past. The time before that was prehistory. There were no written records. But there are remains – fossils, bits of stone and bone, ornaments and cave paintings, pottery and glass. From these leftovers we can piece together how people lived, and how they began to change the world.

Walking on two legs

In Tanzania, Africa, fossil-hunters have found footprints 3.5 million years old. They were made by two-legged creatures who walked like us. The prints are just like the ones you would make when you walk on damp sand at the seaside. They were probably made by ape-humans called *Australopithecus*.

'Lucy', who lived in Africa about 3.2 million years ago, was one of these creatures. Apes usually walk on four legs. Lucy's fossil skeleton shows that she stood upright and walked on two legs, like us. This left her front legs free to become arms, for carrying and making things, such as tools.

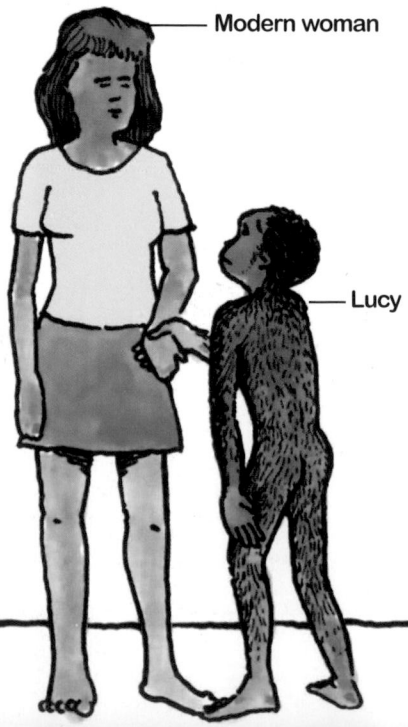

Tools

The first tools were hand-sized rocks and pebbles, chipped into a sharp edge. They were made in Africa over 2 million years ago. Then came our distant cousin *Homo habilis*, or 'Handy Man'. Its tools were used to kill, cut up and skin animals for food. This was the beginning of the early Stone Age.

Gradually the tools got better, sharper and more varied. By half a million years ago more types of humans, such as *Homo erectus*, had learned to make stone hand-axes, scrapers, cutters and chisels. These people hunted many animals, like deer and rhinos.

Fire

Some of the *Homo erectus* people lived in caves, in what is now China. In winter it was icy and snowy. But they weren't cold, because they used fire. Learning to control and use fire was another fantastic step forward – after learning to walk.

Fossilised ashes, and burned wood and bones, show that those ancient humans had fires in their cave homes. They used the fires to keep warm and to cook foods such as meats, berries and fruits. They may have used flaming torches to frighten away wild animals who tried to steal their meal!

Clothes

The earliest humans, such as *Homo habilis*, lived in Africa. They probably had hairy bodies, and the weather was warm, so they had little need for clothes.

Our own species, *Homo sapiens*, appeared about 180,000 years ago. They looked just like us, and they spread from Africa to colder places, such as Europe. They found that the fur coats of skinned animals, draped over their shoulders, kept them warm. Tie a length of creeper around the waist, to stop the fur slipping off, and – hey presto, the first clothes! At last, these folk could go out hunting mammoths on a winter's day in the Ice Age!

More than 30,000 years ago, in Europe and Western Asia, people were sewing fur skins with bone needles and sinew threads. They made fitted cloaks, tunics and leggings. By 20,000 years ago, in what's now the Czech Republic, cloth was being woven.

Art

Around 100,000 years ago carved mammoth's teeth were being worn by people, maybe as good-luck charms. Small statues and models of wild animals were being made by the early Europeans, the Cro-Magnons, about 30,000 years ago.

Cave markings probably go back over 250,000 years. Some of the most beautiful cave paintings are from about 15-20,000 years ago, in Altamira (Spain) and Lascaux (France). They showed how people appreciated beauty and decoration, and they had more spare time to mess around with paints!

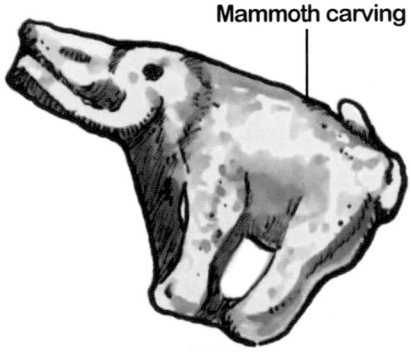

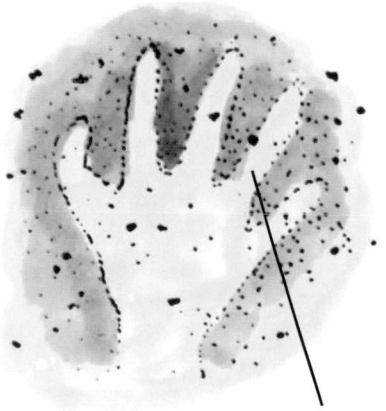

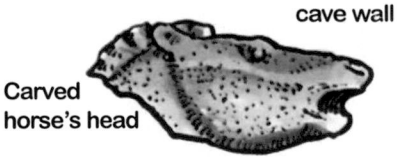

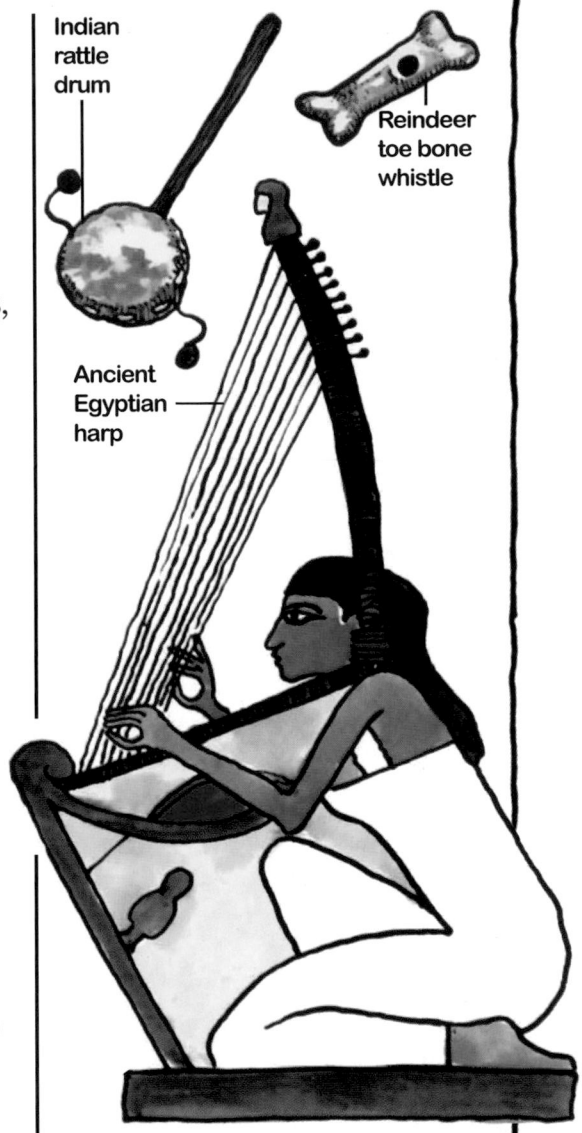

Music

With the beginning of art also came the earliest music. In French caves, there are footprints made by dancers from more than 20,000 years ago, and bones carved to make whistles and drumsticks. One bone from a reindeer's toe, found in northern Europe, makes a beautiful flute sound when you blow over the hole in it. The people probably sang and chanted, too. By the time of Ancient Egypt, 6,000 years ago, musicians played flutes, harps and many other instruments.

Worship

Why bother with art and music? In the tough prehistoric world, weren't they a waste of time?

In the beginning, it's likely that art and music were mixed up with some form of worship and religion. This may have started as a form of remembrance, at the funeral of a loved one. Around 60,000 years ago, in present-day Iraq, people carefully buried their dead. They placed stone tools and animal horns by the body, and scattered flower petals on the grave. Another form of worship was praying for success in the hunt.

Why did people invent spirits, gods and prophets? Maybe they wanted to explain mysterious happenings. Gods could watch over people and bring them rewards for living a good life. Also, the 'chosen ones' who were in touch with the gods, such as priests and scribes, often had great power over the rest of the people! An early prophet of historical times was Zoraster of Persia, around 3,500 years ago.

Jericho, an early city

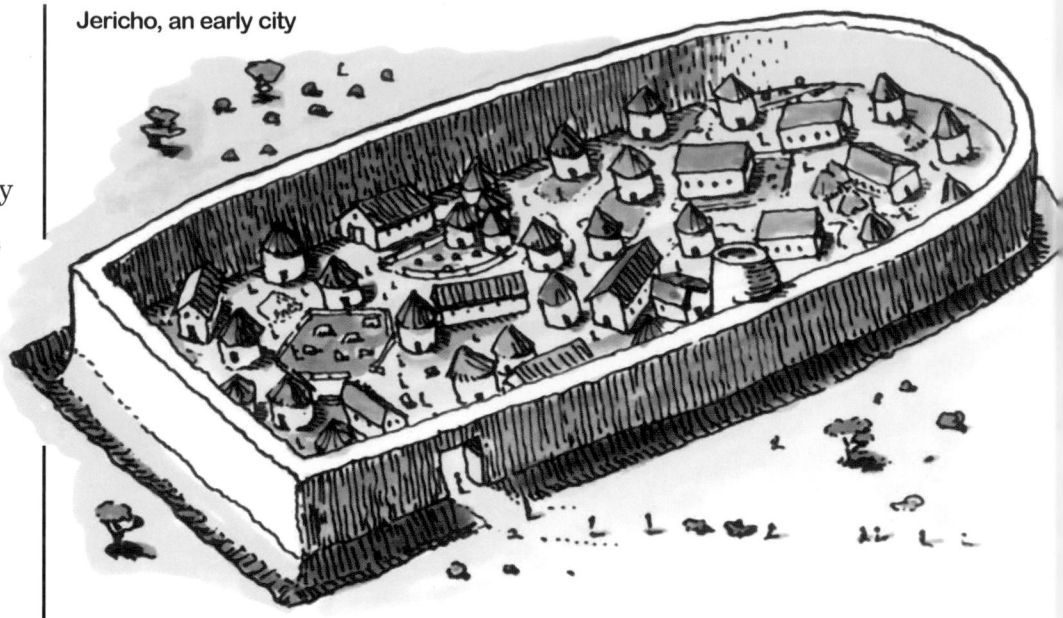

Towns

Caves were cold, dark and draughty. Tents of animal skins and leafy branches could be blown away. Over 10,000 years ago, people discovered that clay could be shaped and dried into bricks and stuck together. The first building sites were invented, as people began to live in simple brick buildings.

Jericho, near the Dead Sea in the Middle East, was an early city. It dates from about 11,000 years ago. By 9,000 years ago it had an outer wall over 5 metres high to keep out – anyone.

Why did people want to live together in a town? They could help each other, share the work, and develop their own skills. They could also defend themselves against dangerous animals and unfriendly people!

The first towns existed before widespread farming. So it's likely that they grew up as trading centres. But the countryside was about to change forever. Farming soon came on the scene.

Farming

The earliest people got their food by hunting wild beasts and searching for nuts and berries. It was dangerous, tiring and boring.

Some time before 10,000 years ago, people in the Middle East decided they wanted a change. They began to tame animals and plant seeds. The tamed animals, such as goats and sheep, did not run away or fight. They gave milk, meat and wool instead. The seeds, like wheat and barley, grew into nourishing food crops. It was the start of farming and an easier, more settled life.

Wines and beers

Many fruits make alcohol as they rot naturally. In the search for interesting foods, some brave people tasted rotting fruit – and they soon felt happy and giggly. They were the first drunks!

Soon grapes were being specially grown to make wine. Besides tasting good, the wine helped to preserve other foods. The alcohol in the wine brought a good feeling, and freedom from worry and pain, although this wore off to leave a hangover headache!

The first wines were fermented in Europe and Mesopotamia, some 10,000 years ago. By about 6,000 years ago, brewers were producing beers too.

Horse-riding

For thousands of years, people had hunted horses for food and skins. Then, more than 6,000 years ago, they started to harness the speed and strength of wild horses. Gradually the horses were tamed so that they could be ridden and pull heavy loads. This happened in Eastern Europe and Central Asia.

A few centuries later, horsemen from the same area rode into battle, speeding past their enemies. Horses were soon spreading to new regions. They carried soldiers and urgent messages, pulled carts and chariots – but often still ended up as food!

Wheels

The first wheels were not on carts, but on potters' tables! In Mesopotamia, over 6,000 years ago, urns and bowls were turned with the help of a rotating solid disc. Then a bright Sumerian had the idea of fixing wheels to a cart. It was no longer such a drag to transport heavy things. Spoked wheels replaced solid wooden ones, and wheels have been rolling ever since.

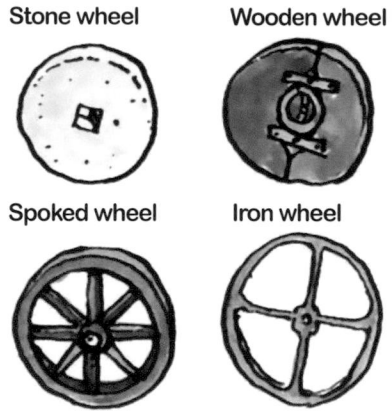

Kurgan horseman

Bronze and iron

Tools of stone, wood and bone tended to break or become blunt. In the search for better materials, people noticed that natural fires melted incredibly hard, shiny stuff out of certain rocks. These were metals.

The Ancient Egyptians found how to smelt and purify copper 5,500 years ago. Mixing it with tin, they started their Bronze Age around 5,000 years ago, although people in Bohemia had been using bronze many years before this. Bronze could be shaped, bent, cast and sharpened easily. The Stone Age was over.

Then some 3,500 years ago, the Hittites learned the more complicated process of purifying iron. Iron took over from bronze. It was harder and it lasted longer. Iron swords and blades were soon hacking off the heads of enemies!

Armies

People have probably always argued and fought each other. But gradually the rewards for a fight increased. The early towns and cities had valuable buildings, farm animals and crops, and works of art. Instead of making all these yourself, why not take someone else's? This was the beginning of organised warfare.

4,000 years ago, the Sumerians had wheeled war chariots. Among the most terrible of the early armies were the Assyrians, who lived 3,000 years ago. They fought with swords, battle-axes, shields, bows and arrows. They tortured and cut up their opponents, and they won many of their battles simply by terrifying the enemy with stories of their horrible cruelty!

Boats

The first sailors may have been driven by natural curiosity. They wanted to know – what's on the other side of the water? Boats were a way to explore and to find new lands. About 50,000 years ago, the first Australians may have travelled there by boat, from South-East Asia.

There are boats in rock paintings over 10,000 years old, in Spain, Scandinavia and Western Asia. Around 5,000 years ago, boats with sails were being blown around Mesopotamian waters. They carried heavy cargoes easily, and the wind power was free!

Through the ages, boats and ships have shaped where we live. Many major cities are ports on seas, lakes and rivers.

Pottery

Clay was 'fired' with great heat to make it strong and hard, over 25,000 years ago in Central Europe. But early purpose-made pots, jars, vats and bowls did not appear until later – including 10,000 years ago in Japan, and 7,000 years ago in the Near East.

Pottery became more widespread as a result of farms. After you produced the food, you needed to carry and store all your extra food for later. Clay vessels were ideal for this. Pots also allowed people to carry water from wells or rivers to their homes.

Glass

The Mesopotamians learned how to heat sand and other chemicals to make glass beads, almost 6,000 years ago. There was an early glassworks in Egypt 3,200 years ago. And around 2,000 years ago, Phoenicians learned how to 'blow' molten (melted) glass to make hollow jars and vases.

Glass was hard, smooth and easily cleaned. It became popular for ornaments and for storing food and drink – and you could see what was inside the jar!

(Glass windows, to keep out the wind and rain, have only become common in the past few hundred years.)

The rule of the law

Unwritten rules, handed down by word of mouth, have probably been around for as long as humans could talk. In nomadic peoples, if a disagreement broke out, one group could simply move away from the other.

Towns and cities changed this. People wanted to stay in their homes, with their valuable possessions. Arguments and fights could start more easily. By 5,000 years ago, civilisations in Egypt, Mesopotamia, India and China had rules and laws. The idea of the laws was to keep people in order and make life peaceful. Punishment was harsh. You could lose your arm just for stealing bread!

Schools

Sometimes, you may think that school is boring. But imagine being taught nothing at all!

For thousands of years, people's lives were taken up with hunting, collecting plant food, and generally surviving. Children learned from their elders – or they perished.

As life became more complicated, new and more specialised jobs developed. The Ancient Egyptians and Sumerians had schools to teach their future politicians, priests and builders. The children learned about astronomy, writing, mathematics, architecture and government.

Votes for the people

Through the ages, many civilisations have been ruled by one person, such as a pharaoh, king, queen, emperor or priest. About 2,500 years ago, the Ancient Greeks began a system where the ordinary people could choose who governed them. This is called democracy, from the Greek words *demos*, meaning 'the people', and *kratia*, which means 'rule'.

Today, many countries have democratic governments. The people vote for their leaders, who make decisions that affect us all. We, through them, can change the world!

THE TOILET

Yes, it's true. Once upon a time, there were no toilets. People left their – er, what shall we call them – body wastes behind the nearest bush. When there were fewer people, human droppings did not get in the way. They sure would today!

In the distant past, people did what animals do. They left their body wastes in the countryside, in a hole, or in a local river. The wastes were eaten by maggots, worms and dung beetles, and rotted away in the usual manner.

Gradually, there were more people, in towns and cities. The countryside got farther away. Body wastes began to pile up in smelly, rotting heaps, polluting the water and spreading disease. Something had to be done.

ROMAN LATRINE

Wooden seats

Shallow channel

Water-filled trough

The hole in the floor

In ancient times, people had special seats with holes in, and pots beneath to catch the wastes. The pots were emptied outside. This happened in ancient Sumeria, Egypt and India, thousands of years ago. Over 2,000 years ago, the Romans had simple toilets. Wastes fell through a hole in the floor into a sewer, where running water carried them away.

Look out below!

However, most people did not bother with toilets. They dug a hole at the end of the garden or in a field, and used that. As it filled up, they covered it with soil and dug another one. At night, they used a chamber-pot kept under the bed.

In castles, special holes were made in a wall or tower next to the moat. The wastes fell, plop, into the water of the moat. This seat was called a garderobe.

Garderobe

Moat

Flushing

In the flush toilet, or water closet (WC), water from a tank swishes the wastes into the sewer. John Harington, godson of Queen Elizabeth I, had the idea in 1589. But hardly any houses had a water supply to fill the tank, or a drain where it could be emptied.

Two hundred years later, piped water and drains were more common. Alexander Cumming, a London watchmaker, designed a flush toilet. In 1778, inventor Joseph Bramah made a better one, with a cast iron bowl and a flap that opened into the drains. Bramah's closet was the first big-selling toilet.

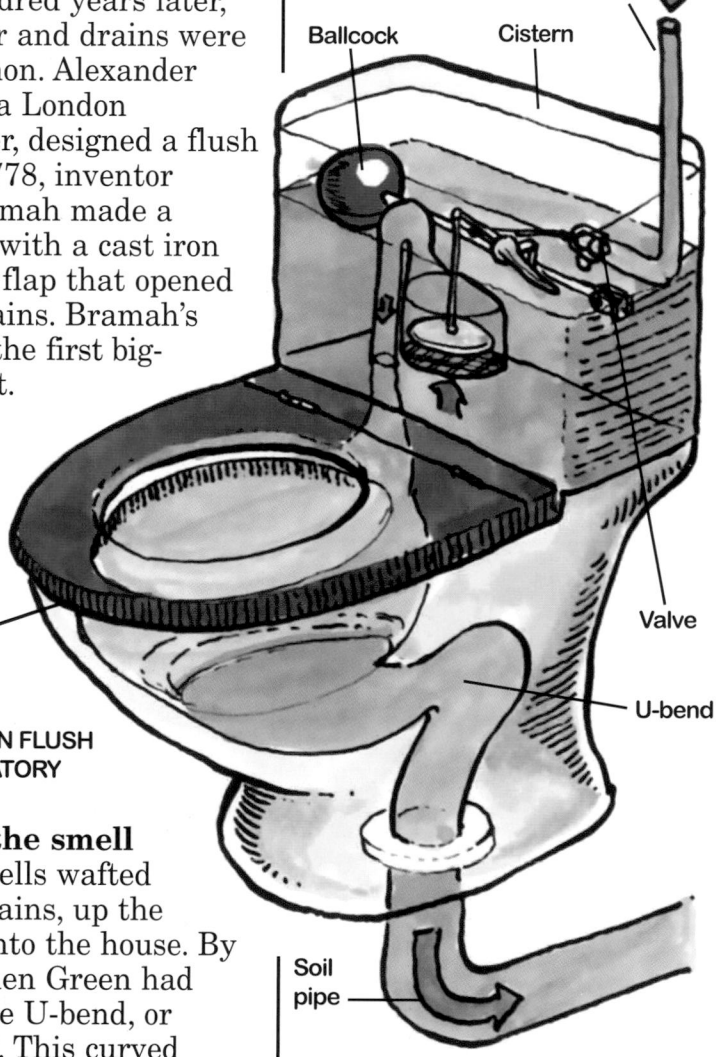

MODERN FLUSH LAVATORY

Stopping the smell

Terrible smells wafted from the drains, up the toilet and into the house. By 1849, Stephen Green had designed the U-bend, or 'water trap'. This curved piece of pipe, between bowl and drain, was always partly filled by water from the last flush. The water stopped smells coming in.

About the same time, ceramic (porcelain) bowls became popular. Their very smooth, shiny surface was easier to clean than iron.

Down the pan

Next was Doulton's pedestal water closet, invented in 1888. The water was stored in a tank, or cistern, on the wall, high above the toilet bowl, or pan. Pull the chain and water rushed down the pipe, around the bowl, through the trap and into the sewer.

In about 1915, a new toilet design used the suction power of the siphon. It washed water strongly but quietly around the bowl. The water cistern could be placed much lower, just above the bowl. The all-singing, all-dancing, low-level flush toilet had arrived.

So that's where it came from...

• In the last century, one of the most famous English 'sanitary engineers' was Thomas Crapper. Sounds familiar? His company made toilets, washbasins and baths.

• The toilet became known as the privy, because it was a hidden and private place.

• The toilet is also known as the loo, powder room, water closet, bog, rest room and john.

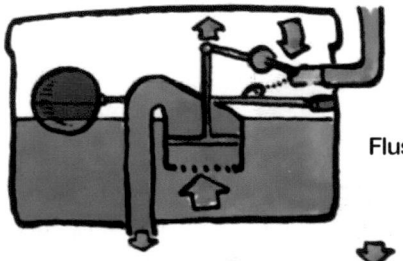

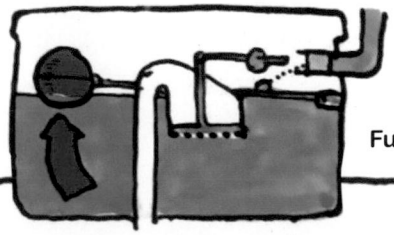

THE BLAST FURNACE

How would you like to pull apart your food with your hands and eat it with your fingers – at every meal? Knives and forks are just a couple of the thousands of things made from steel. Which is made from iron. And iron could only be made in large quantities once the blast furnace was invented.

In the beginning, people used stone, bone and wood. They wore out quickly. Then came the Iron Age, described on page 9. Iron was hard, and it could be melted, shaped, hammered and cast. But the problem was getting it out of iron ores, the natural rocks which contained it. For centuries, it was a slow process, and the iron itself was not very pure.

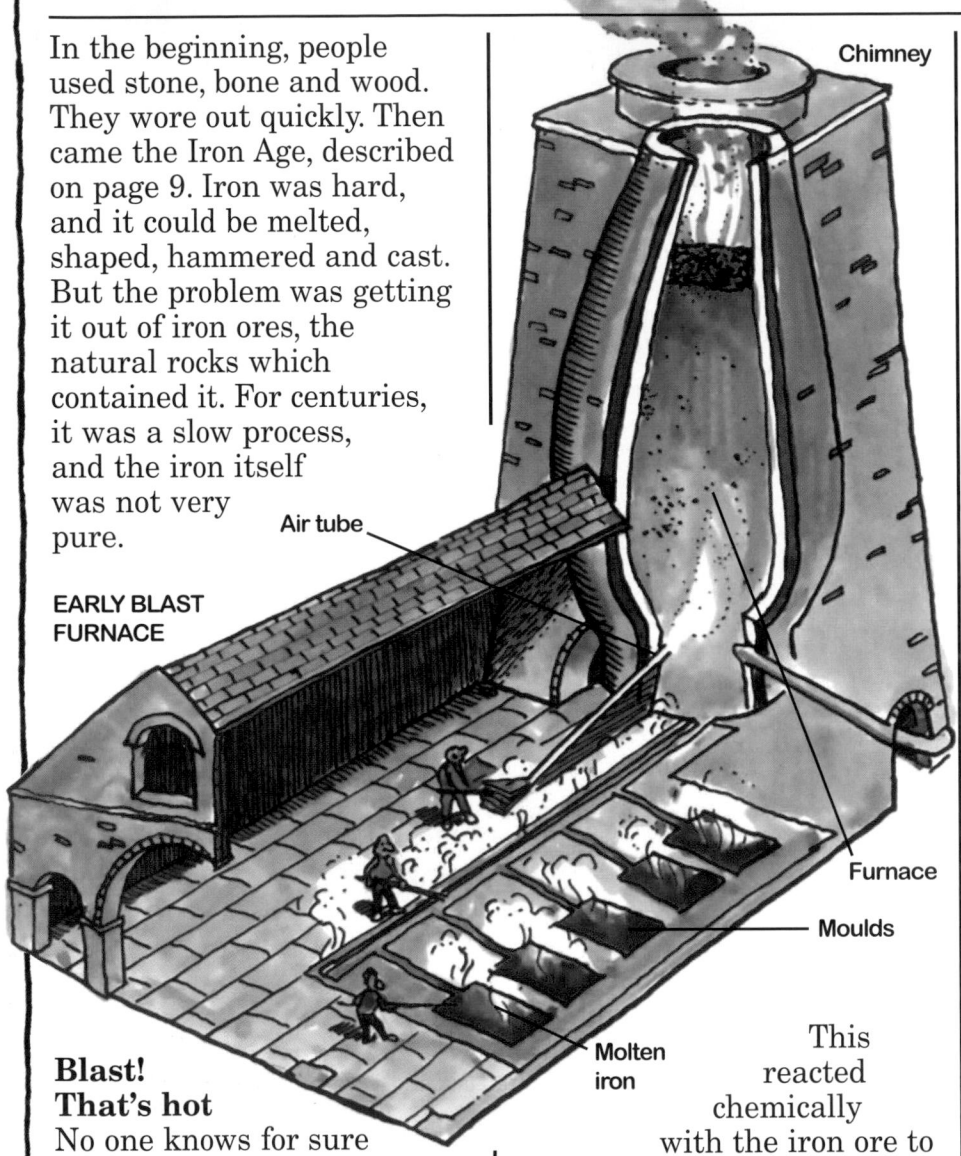

EARLY BLAST FURNACE

Blast! That's hot

No one knows for sure who invented the first blast furnace, but it happened during the Middle Ages. The idea was to heat charcoal, iron ore and limestone in a huge stone oven, at more than 1,000°C.

The charcoal burned with intense heat. As it burned it made carbon monoxide gas. This reacted chemically with the iron ore to remove the rocky bits and leave pure iron.

The limestone absorbed the leftover bits to form slag, which was poured away.

The basic process was brought about by a blast of air blown up through the furnace to keep it glowing – the blast furnace.

More and more iron

By about 1840 iron-makers discovered that anthracite, a type of coal, burned hotter than charcoal, and if they pre-heated the blast of air, the furnace burned even better. The modern blast furnace was born. In the 1870s, coke replaced anthracite.

In those early days, a blast furnace made about 30 tonnes of iron each week. Today's blast furnace has a huge chimney-stack 30 metres high. It burns at 2,000°C, and makes more than 10,000 tonnes of iron every day, seven days a week. Iron is the commonest engineering metal. We couldn't do without it.

Iron facts

- Over nine-tenths of iron goes to make steel, for buildings, cars, trains, engines, machines, gear wheels, and of course knives and forks.
- The Empire State Building in New York has a steel framework weighing 55,000 tonnes.
- The world's tallest skyscraper, the Burj Khalifa in Dubai, has just 4,000 tonnes of steel.

THE ROAD

Without roads, life would be very limited. It could take days to visit friends 'down the road' – or rather, across the countryside – on bumpy, puddle-filled cart tracks. Without roads, our cars and motorbikes and trucks would have to stay in the garage!

About 5,000 years ago, people in the Middle East tried to improve their worn trackways by covering them with flat stones and gravel. But the first proper road-builders were the Romans, more than 2,000 years ago. Their 80,000 kilometres of roads criss-crossed lands of the Roman Empire, from North Africa to Scotland, from Spain to the Middle East.

Roman roads had strong foundations, stone-paved surfaces, and good drains so that they did not flood. They cut straight lines across the countryside. Roman soldiers, chariots and supply carts could get quickly from place to place.

Modern roads

During the Dark Ages, most Roman roads crumbled away. The main routes became muddy horse-and-cart tracks. In the 1700s British engineers such as John McAdam and Thomas Telford began to build roads with strong stone foundations, a layer of hard-packed smaller stones over that, and a layer of hard-packed gravel on top.

With the coming of cars and trucks, from about 1900, the gravel topping was too loose. Modern roads have a variety of surfaces made from thick, black, gooey asphalt and tar, along with sand, sandstone, gravel, concrete and other tough materials.

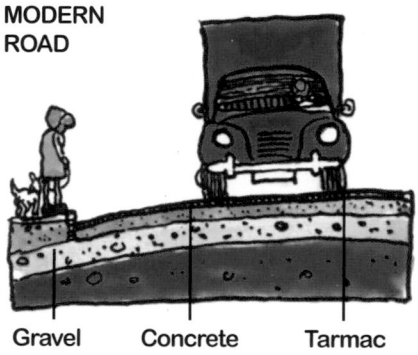

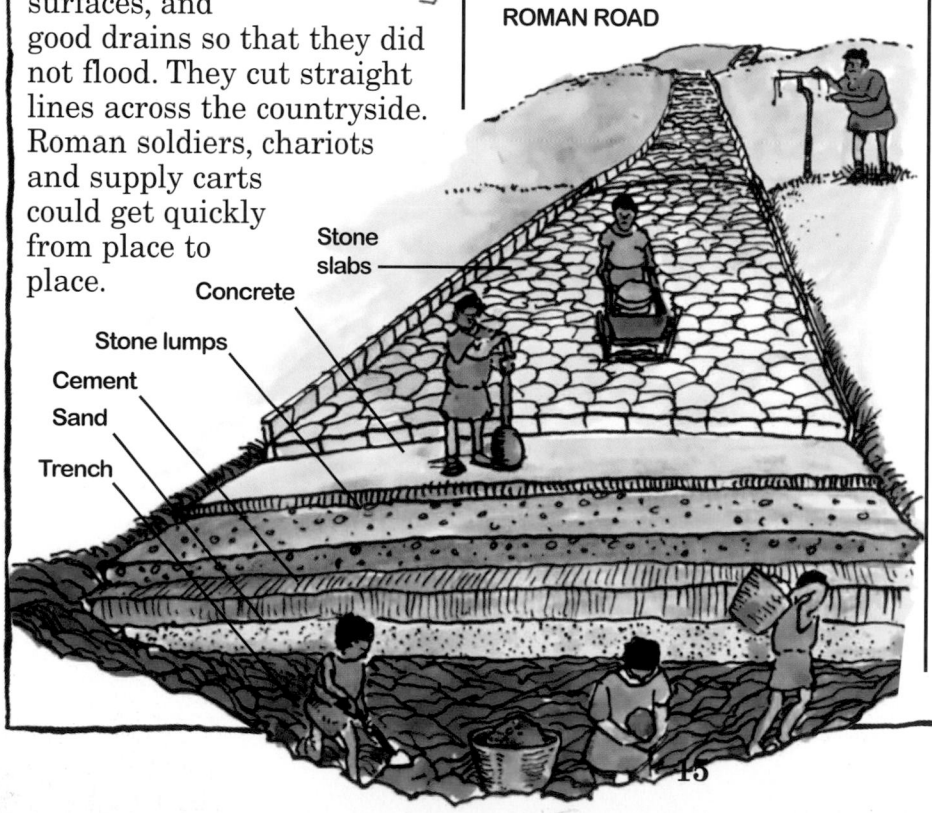

Well, I never knew that...

- Roads were not only for wheeled vehicles. In South America, the Inca people never discovered wheeled transport, yet five hundred years ago they had more than 20,000 kilometres of roads stretching across the continent. These were walked mainly by people and their load-carrying animals – llamas!
- 'Tarmac' (tarmacadam) is a road surface of crushed stones and sand mixed with tar. It is named after the tar in it, and the man who invented it, John 'Macadam' McAdam.

THE CLOCK

Tick-tock, tick-tock, tick ... RRRRRING. Drat, the alarm clock. School at nine. Music club at four. Eat at six. My favourite TV show at seven. Why does bedtime always come too early? Time, and clocks, rule our lives.

In the old days, life was slower. There were no clocks. You'd tell friends you'd see them a day or two after new moon, perhaps before sundown.

Early time-keeping machines were very simple. Water dripped steadily through a hole. Marks on a candle slowly burned away. The shadow moved regularly around a sundial. It didn't matter – hardly anyone kept accurate time.

Sundial

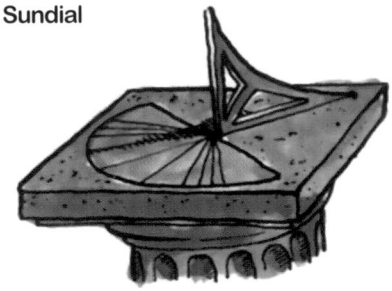

Escaping time

From about AD 1000, inventors made mechanical clocks. The fall of a weight on a chain was controlled by a bar with a point on each end that rocked to and fro. Each rock let a gear wheel turn, or 'escape', by one tooth – the verge escapement.

Famous Dutch scientist Christiaan Huygens designed clocks which used the regular swing of a pendulum, in the 1650s.

Around this time, exploring sailors wanted better clocks. Their navigation depended on taking readings at the right time, from the Sun, Moon and stars. Inventors came up with more accurate clocks called chronometers, or 'time-measurers'.

Christiaan Huygens

Good timing

By the 1700s, the wind-up clockwork clock was basically the same as we know it today. Modern clocks have electric motors, or vibrating quartz crystals. The best lose only 1 second in a million years!

We run our lives by the clock. How would you like it if your birthday party was three days late?

Digital watch

Whoops! Not a good idea

• For many years, wristwatches were worn only by women. Men liked bigger pocket-watches. But in World War One, soldiers realised wristwatches were useful. Soon men wore them too.

Watch pinned to sleeve

THE PIANO

Music fills our world with beautiful sounds. It is a career for some, and a pleasure for millions. Almost every music room or concert hall has a piano. Guitars may be popular today, but the piano has been the main instrument, for players and composers, for almost three centuries.

Listen to the music charts every week and probably at least half of the songs feature a piano. Almost all major pieces of classical music were written on the piano too. It's ideal for playing a tune with one hand and backing with the other.

Hit, not plucked

The forerunner of the piano was the harpsichord, where the strings inside are plucked. In Italy in the early 1700s, Bartolomeo Cristofori made a new version. The strings were hit by small cloth-covered wooden hammers.

He called it a harpsichord with *piano e forte*, which means 'soft and loud'. The player made loud sounds by pressing the keys hard, and quiet ones by pressing them softly – which the earlier harpsichord could not do. The new instrument became known as the pianoforte, and eventually, the piano.

Cast-iron pianos

Early pianos were lightweight and not very loud. By the 1770s a new design, the English action, let the hammers hit the keys much harder, for more forceful playing.

In 1825, American Alpheus Babcock designed a cast-iron frame, to take the tremendous force of the stretched metal strings. Pianos could be stronger and louder. They have hardly changed since. But they have changed all types of music, from classical to hip-hop.

EARLY SQUARE PIANO

Strings

Wooden case

Sounding board

Hammer

Five octave keyboard

GRAND PIANO

How the piano works

Press a piano key, and lots of levers move inside. The jack releases the hammer, which hits the string, bounces back, and is caught by the check and repetition lever. If you keep the key down, the damper stays away from the string and the note carries on and on.

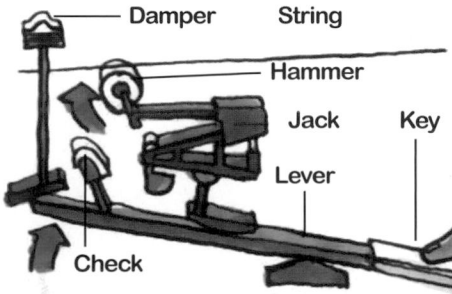

THE PLOUGH

How about a snack? Peanut butter sandwich, maybe? Go out and find some wild wheat, grind its seeds into flour, make your own bread. And find some wild peanuts while you're out. Without ploughs and planting, every mealtime would be like this.

About 9,000 years ago in the Middle East, the first farmers probably had bad backs. They discovered that if they broke up the ground first, and got rid of weeds, the seeds they planted would grow better. They used deer antlers or sharp sticks to hoe the ground. Back-breaking work!

By 6,000 years ago, the Egyptians carved a strong piece of sharpened wood, and pushed or pulled it through the soil. The power came from people or oxen. It was a simple plough, to break up the soil before planting crops.

The Greeks and Romans added a metal tip to the main plough blade, the ploughshare, so it did not wear away so quickly.

Coultes and mouldboards

The Middle Ages, around 1000-1200 AD, saw several improvements. Wheels were added to steady the plough for easier control. A metal cutting blade was added, too. This was the coulter, which sliced the earth in front of the main ploughshare. Then came the curved mouldboard, which turned the soil over, to give a fresh surface for planting.

Ploughs made completely of iron appeared around 1800. Oxen or horses still pulled them.

At the start of the last century, along chugged the tractor. It became so powerful that it could pull lots of plough blades, in a gang-plough, through even the heaviest soil. Now a tractor driver can plough more in a day than 50 Ancient Egyptians could in a week!

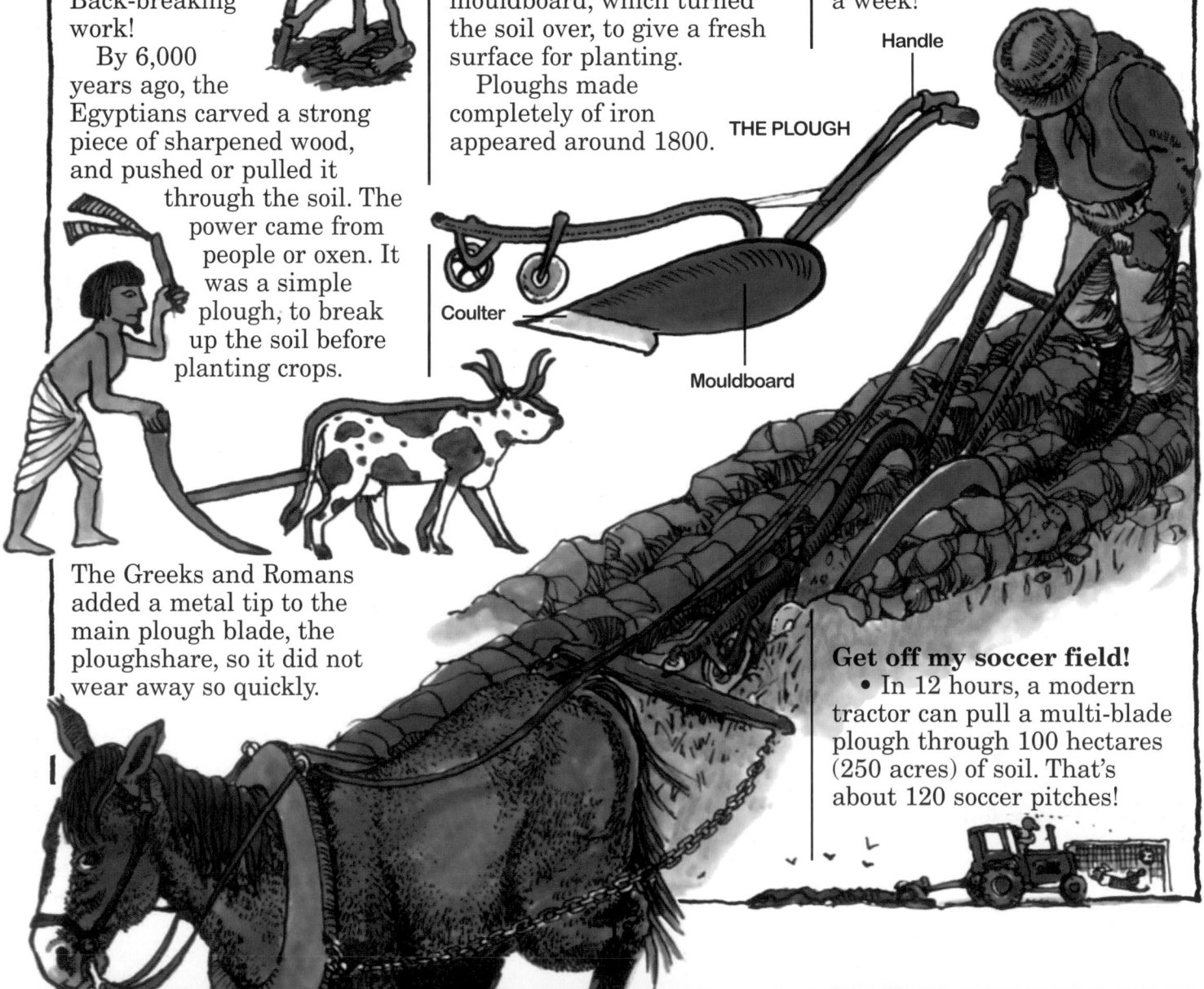

Get off my soccer field!

• In 12 hours, a modern tractor can pull a multi-blade plough through 100 hectares (250 acres) of soil. That's about 120 soccer pitches!

THE COMBINE HARVESTER

Imagine a harvest scene in the old days ... Golden autumn sunset over the fields ... Farm workers spending all day cutting and stacking bundles of wheat ... The next job is threshing, then baling the straw. Hang on, this sounds like hard work! Let's invent the combine harvester.

Harvests were hard work. You had to:

Reap When the crop ripened it was reaped, or cut, usually with sickles.

Thresh It was bashed with long-handled flails, to separate the grain (seeds), chaff (unwanted bits) and straw (stems).

Load The grain was loaded into wagons, for the mill or grain store.

Bale The straw was tied into bundles, for animal bedding and food.

Combining jobs

Today, you have to: *Combine*. This huge multi-purpose machine combines the harvesting tasks. It does the jobs of up to 100 farm workers. It can harvest wheat, barley, rye or oats. With a few changes it can deal with soy beans, rice and many other crops.

Tractors pulled the first combines over American prairie fields in the 1920s. Next they were made with their own engines. They were the latest in a long line of farm machines that took the hard work – but also the romance and employment – out of harvest time.

Whoops! Not a good idea, at the time

• Andrew Meikle invented a mechanical thresher in the mid-1800s. Far from being thankful, farm workers rioted. They realised it could do their work quickly, and they relied on threshing as a winter job.

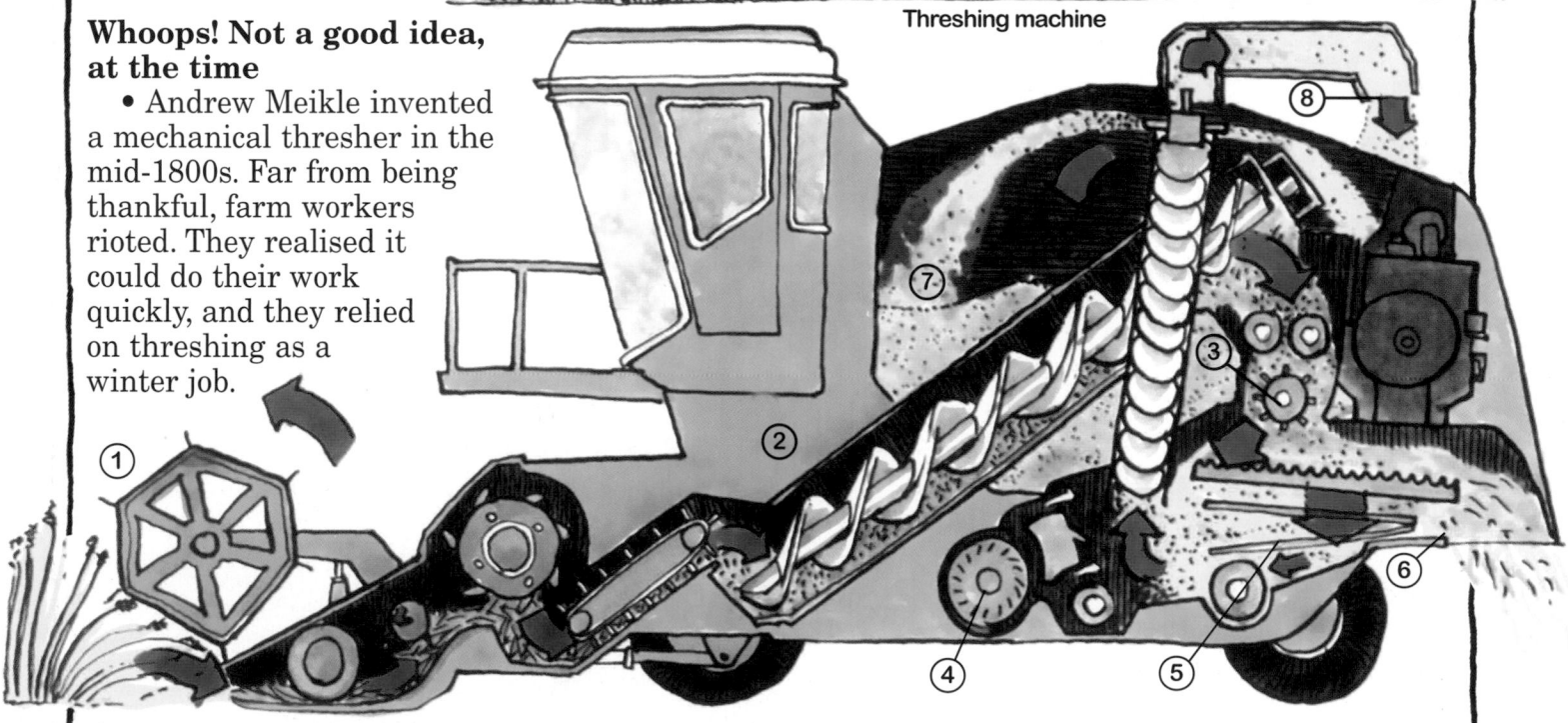

How the combine works

1 Reel pulls crop against cutting bar.
2 Screw-shaped auger pulls crop towards threshing cylinder.
3 Threshing cylinder separates grain, chaff and straw.
4 Fan blows away chaff.
5 Straw walker separates straw.
6 Straw is thrown out the back.
7 Grain is stored in a holding tank.
8 Grain empties into a truck or wagon alongside.

THE SAIL

'Ahoy, shipmates! There's a storm brewin'. Reef the mains'l (see note 1, below) and sheet the jib (2), or we won't splice the mainbrace (3) later!'
Before steamships, trains, trucks and planes, the sailing ship opened up new lands and trade routes around the globe. Today, these ships are used mainly for fun and racing.

The early sailing ships probably crossed the Mediterranean over 5,000 years ago. One rectangular sail hung from a crosswise pole called a spar, held on an upright pole, the mast. Wind power was free, and less tiring than paddles!

Phoenician merchant ship

Roman warship

The Ancient Egyptians were great sailors. So were the Phoenicians, with their galleys over 30 metres (100 feet) long. When the wind dropped, rows of oarsmen went into action. The Ancient Greeks and Romans used sailing ships to carry armies and supplies around their empires.

The golden age of sail
Through the Middle Ages and towards modern times, many different kinds of sailing ships were developed. Great wooden warships such as galleons had up to four masts and a dozen sails. They decided the fate of nations.

Fastest were the clippers, in the mid-1800s. They brought tea and spices from the Far East to Europe, and sailed to America and Australia. Some had over 20 sails. The clipper *Lightning* went 700 kilometres (435 miles) in one day. Few modern ships could go that fast!

A lot of sail
• The sails of British battleship HMS *Sultan*, built in 1871, covered 3,150 square metres. That's the area of 12 tennis courts.

1 Reef the mains'l – Gather in part of the main sail, to reduce its area.

2 Sheet the jib – Pull the rope on the small triangular sail at the front.

3 Splice the mainbrace – Get out the rum and the other drinks!

THE SCREW

'Eureka! (I've found it!)' cried Archimedes of Ancient Greece, as he jumped from his bath and ran through the street. He had discovered Archimedes' principle, which has nothing to do with screws. But Archimedes supposedly invented the screw, too. It is used for irrigation, joining things, pushing along ships and aeroplanes, and opening wine bottles!

Over 2,000 years ago, people used screws to water their fields. Tar-covered wooden strips, in a corkscrew (helix) shape, were put in a tight-fitting wooden tube. A person turned the screw to raise water up the tube, lifting it from a lake or river, up to the fields. Still in use today, this device is the Archimedean screw.

Archimedean screw

Screws, nuts and bolts

In the 1600s, carpenters and craftsmen began to make their own screws, for fixing parts together. The woodscrew's narrow point gets wider, and its head has a slot for the screwdriver. In 1841, Joseph Whitworth designed standard sizes for screws, and these were mass-produced.

Screw

Engineers also use fixing devices known as bolts and nuts. Without screws, nuts and bolts, our world really would fall apart!

Ships and planes

The first ship powered by a screw, or screw-propeller, was made in America in about 1804. It had sails, too, just in case. Screw-propellers were more effective than thrashing, energy-wasting paddles. 1843 saw the *Great Britain*, designed by Isambard Kingdom Brunel. It was the first big ship with a screw-propeller and an iron hull.

The Wright brothers used the same principle, but in air, not water, for the first aeroplane (page 42). All early planes, and most small planes today, have propellers or 'airscrews'.

The *Great Britain*

Screwdriver

Propeller

Bolt

Nut

Paddle versus screw

• In 1845 the British Navy organised a tug-o'-war between a paddle-driven ship, the *Alecto*, and a screw-propeller ship, the *Rattler*. The screw won and soon took over from paddle wheels.

THE TELESCOPE AND MICROSCOPE

Do you believe that the Moon is made of green cheese, and that germs don't exist? If you had a telescope and a microscope, you could see for yourself. Telescopes look at outer space, to reveal the mysteries of the Universe. Microscopes look into inner space, to show us what our own bodies are made of.

Many inventors and scientists messed about with curved pieces of glass, called lenses. From the 1200s, lenses of various strengths were used in spectacles. Two lenses, specially shaped and put near to each other, make distant things look bigger and nearer. This was probably discovered by Hans Lippershey in Holland, in about 1608.

Early spectacles

Within a year, the famous Italian Galileo heard about the newly invented telescope, and made his own versions. They magnified up to 30 times. He scanned the dark skies and discovered mountains on the Moon, dark spots on the fiery Sun, and moons going round the planet Jupiter.

Galileo

GALILEO'S TELESCOPE

Types of telescopes

In about 1757 a London optician, John Dollond, sandwiched two lenses closely together. These compound lenses gave better, clearer images.

In 1668 the great Isaac Newton designed a telescope with a curved mirror in place of one lens. This was called a reflector. Today, the biggest optical telescopes are reflectors. They peer deep into space – in fact, some are *in* space. The James Webb space telescope, replacement for the Hubble one, will tell us even more about our Moon and Sun, planets and stars, comets and asteroids, and how the Universe began.

Isaac Newton

REFRACTING LENS TELESCOPE

Telescope focused by moving extensions

Extension tubes

Eyepiece lens

James Webb Space Telescope

SIMPLE REFRACTING (LENS) TELESCOPE

Eyepiece lens

Convex lens

Mirror

NEWTONIAN REFLECTOR

Eyepiece

Mirror

Seeing the invisible

Around 1590, Dutch lens-maker Zacharias Janssen also put two lenses near to each other. He noticed that a tiny thing at one end looked much bigger from the other end – provided the lenses were the right distance apart.

Scientists showed an interest. They realised that a whole tiny world was waiting to be discovered. In 1655, Robert Hooke first used the word 'cell' for a microscopic part of a living thing, in his book Micrographia ('Small Drawings'). Hooke showed that tiny creatures such as ants had a heart, stomach and other body parts – just like bigger animals, but smaller!

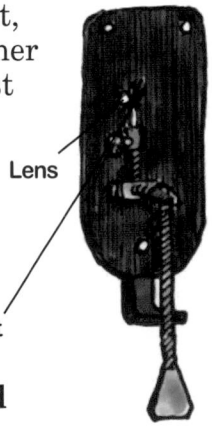

LEEUWENHOEK'S MICROSCOPE

Draper turned lens-maker

By the 1680s Anton van Leeuwenhoek, in Holland, had made fascinating discoveries through the microscope. His home-made versions could magnify over 250 times. Through them he saw new wonders such as red blood cells, tiny one-celled amoebas, the eggs of fleas, insect eyes, and stacks of cells in the thinnest plant leaf.

Anton van Leeuwenhoek

After Leeuwenhoek, many people looked through microscopes. The science of microbiology began. Soon people were looking at germs, and working out how they invaded the body and caused diseases.

Microscopes became more powerful, with strong lights and changeable lenses that could magnify over one thousand times. Today, medicine and biology would be lost without microscopes.

BENCH MICROSCOPE

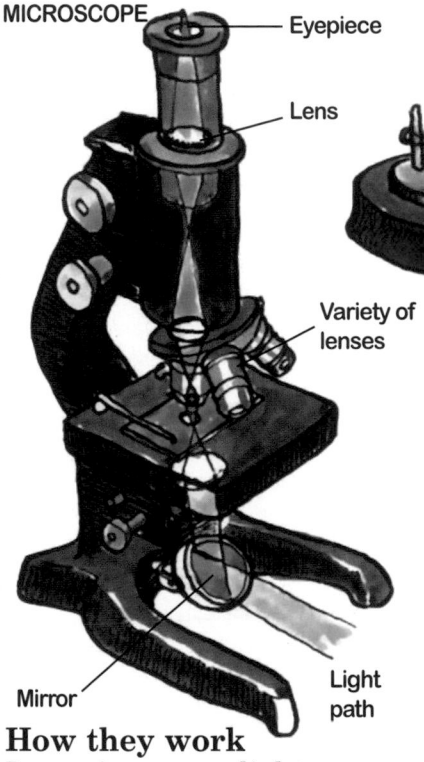

How they work

In a microscope, light waves from the tiny and nearby object are bent inwards by the convex (bulging) lens. They are bent again at the second lens, the eyepiece, so that you see a clear and enlarged view.

In a telescope, much the same happens, but the light waves come from far, far away, so they are parallel when they reach the telescope.

EARLY MICROSCOPE

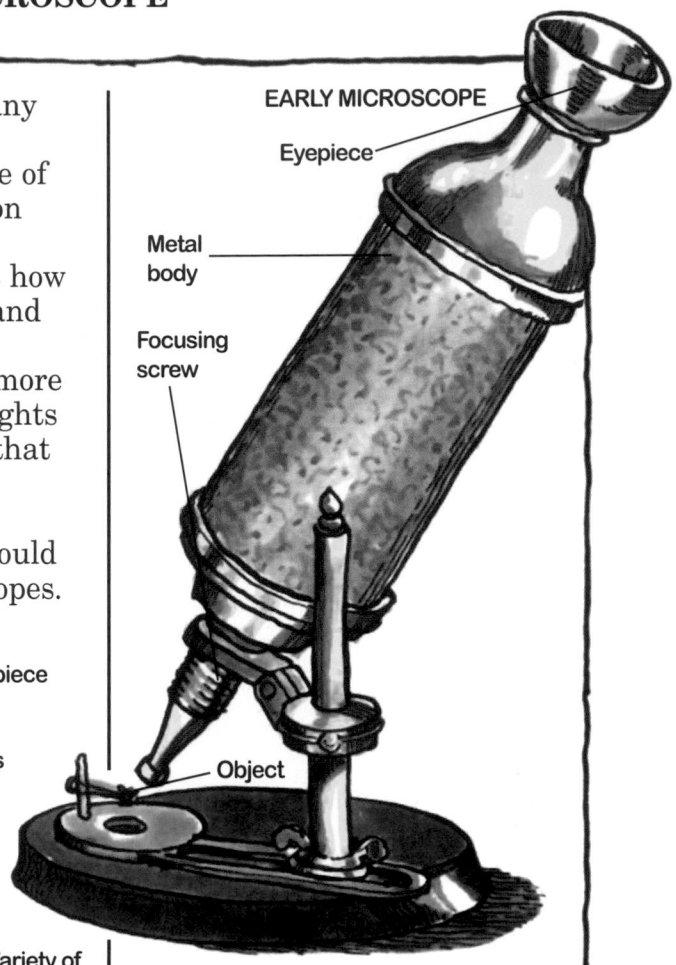

Wow! Big, small, and far-out

- The refracting telescope with the biggest one-piece lens is at the Yerkes Observatory, USA. The lens is 102 centimetres (40 inches) across.
- Electron microscopes use electron beams instead of light rays. They magnify over one million times.
- Radio telescopes detect not light rays, but radio waves from stars, quasars and pulsars. They can 'see' billions of kilometres, to the far side of the Universe.

Radio telescopes

THE PRINTING PRESS

If printing had never been invented, then

...Exactly!!

The year: 1455. The place: Mainz, Germany. The person: Johann Gutenberg. The result: about 300 copies of what we now call the Gutenberg Bible, the first full-length book made on a proper mechanical printing press. It had 1,284 pages, two columns on each page, 42 lines in each column. Fewer than 50 copies survive. We see printed words, drawings and photographs almost everywhere! They are in books, newspapers and magazines, on containers and labels, on billboard posters, even on T-shirts! Printing is central to the way we learn. Imagine life without school textbooks! (Then again, don't.)

Johann Gutenberg

One copy at a time

There was printing five centuries before Gutenberg. In China, shapes of pictures and writing were cut onto wood or stone blocks. Printers coated the block with ink, pressed paper on it, and the ink on the surface area stuck to the paper. They could make many prints from one block.

Early printing block

But each new work needed a new block. So a system was developed with small metal blocks, which could be moved and arranged in different orders. However, the complicated Chinese writing system, with thousands of symbols, meant slow progress.

Early Chinese

There were also hand-made books before Gutenberg. Monks, especially, spent years hand-writing and decorating their letters with pens, one beautiful book at a time.

Moveable type

Gutenberg and his helpers produced hundreds of small metal blocks, each with a raised letter or symbol. The letters for each word could be chosen to set in a frame, to print copies of one page from the book. Then a new set of letters was put into the frame for the next page. And so on, one page at a time.

Metal type blocks

GUTENBERG'S PRESS

Inking the type

Gutenberg Ink Inc.

Another Gutenberg advance was new ink that stuck to the metal type, rather than to the usual carved woodblocks. And another was a powerful pressing machine that squeezed the paper against the inked type. It was adapted from a wine press for squashing grapes!

Because the raised, inked letters were pressed onto paper, the method was called letterpress.

The letters and symbols were called type, and setting them up correctly was typesetting. For a long time they were placed by hand. In 1884 the Linotype machine made a line of type from molten metal that quickly went solid.

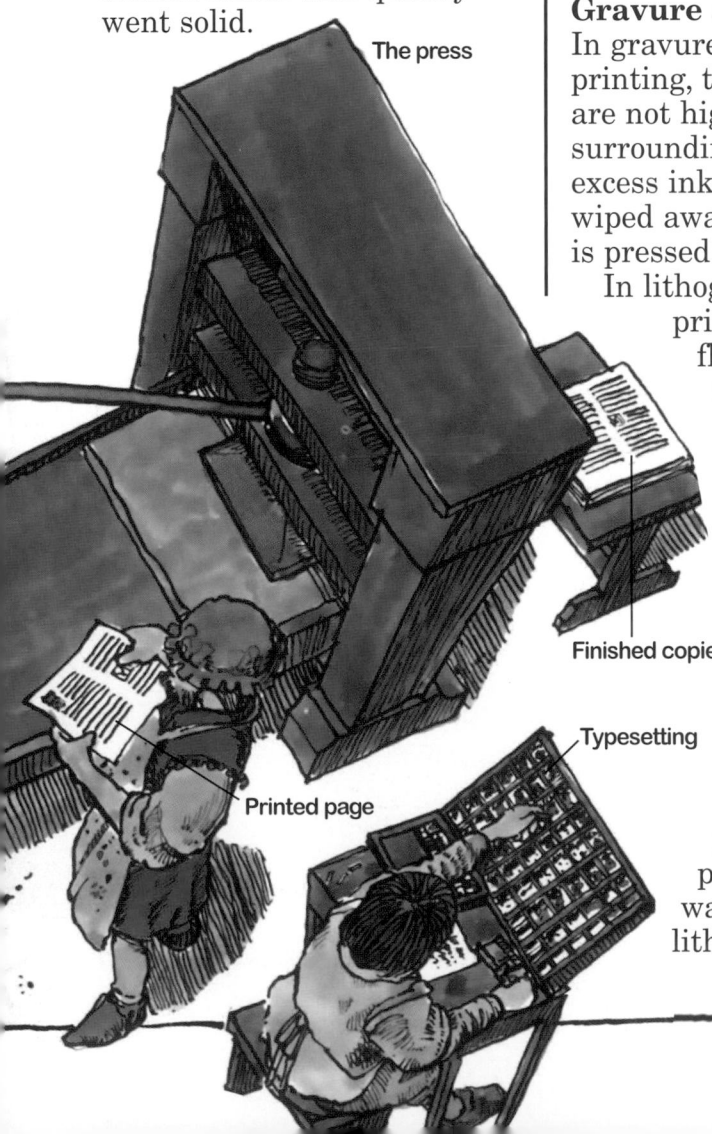

PRINTING PRESS

Computer
Paper feed
Yellow ink feed
Printing plate
Offset roller
Cyan ink feed
Magenta ink feed
Black ink feed

Colour pictures are printed from tiny dots of four ink colours; yellow, cyan (greeny-blue), magenta (reddy-purple) and black. If you don't believe that, look at this page under a magnifying lens.

Friedrich Konig invented the rotary or cylinder press in 1811. It saved the time winding the press up and down for each paper sheet.

Gravure and litho

In gravure or intaglio printing, the areas to print are not higher than their surroundings, but lower. The excess ink is scraped or wiped away before the paper is pressed.

In lithography, the printing surface is flat. But the areas to be printed have their surface changed, so that the oil-based ink sticks only to them, and not to the untreated areas around. 'Litho' was invented in about 1800 by Aloys Senefelder. It is now the most popular kind of printing - this book was printed using litho.

The Age of Learning

Within 50 years of Gutenberg, there were printers in 200 towns around Europe, producing over 15,000 works. The main result was cheaper books. Many more people could buy them, and learn to read and write. Then they bought more books, read them, and learned even more. Schools and education changed forever.

Well I never!

- A printing system at the Lawrence Radiation Laboratory, California, USA, printed the Bible in 65 seconds. That's 773,700 words!

MEDICINE

If you had a headache, would you let someone drill a hole in your skull to release the 'evil spirits'? Medicine started like that! Most people nowadays expect doctors to cure them of life's aches and pains, and to heal serious diseases. Good medical care is sometimes not appreciated. It is just taken for granted.

Medicine began in the mists of prehistory. Some people found that they could cure an illness with a potion of plant juices, or a smear of animal fluids. They were the first doctors.

Some skulls over 10,000 years old have holes bored in them. The bone had grown back after being drilled, so these people must have survived after their 'operation', trepanning.

A few early treatments worked, but many did not. Some were very harmful. Even so, if a medicine worked, people had respect and wonder for the doctor. As a result, doctors became powerful, and some were made into gods.

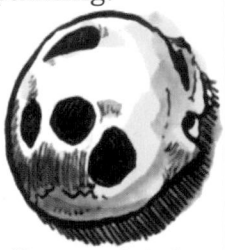

Trepanned skull

The father of medicine

One of the first proper doctors was Hippocrates of Ancient Greece. He tried to rid medicine of magic and superstitions, and make it more scientific. He taught that a doctor's main aim was to help the patient, by finding the cause of an illness, and treating it. The results should be checked, so medicines could be improved. Hippocrates' main ideas are still followed today.

Hippocrates

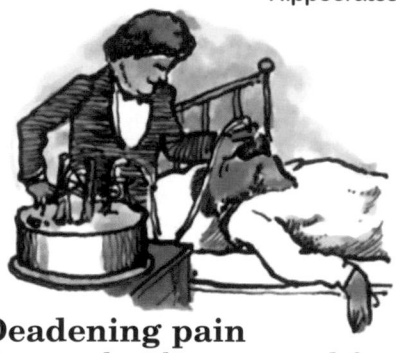

Deadening pain

Surgery has been around for thousands of years. The only way of deadening the pain of the knife and saw was to get the patient very drunk on alcohol. In 1842, American doctor Crawford Long operated on a patient using ether as an anaesthetic, to deaden pain and other sensations. Today we could not imagine even a very small operation without an anaesthetic.

Joseph Lister

Killing germs on the body

Until the 1860s, patients who had operations often suffered and died, because their wounds became infected with germs. British surgeon Joseph Lister began to use antiseptics (germ-killing substances) to clean his operating instruments and the patient's cuts. Within a few years, surgery became much safer.

Alexander Fleming

Killing germs in the body

In 1928, British scientist Alexander Fleming discovered a substance which could kill bacteria (types of germs). It was made by a pinhead-sized mould called *Penicillium*, so he named it penicillin. This was the first antibiotic (bacteria-killing) drug. Many other antibiotics have been discovered, and they have saved millions of lives.

Seeing inside the body

X-rays were discovered by German professor Wilhelm Roentgen in 1895. People were amazed that they could pass through the body, except for bones. Soon X-rays were showing up broken bones and suspicious lumps and bumps.

Doctors now have many methods of seeing into the body. CT and MR scans show inside parts in amazing detail. Thin tubes called endoscopes can be pushed into the body, to examine and photograph the insides.

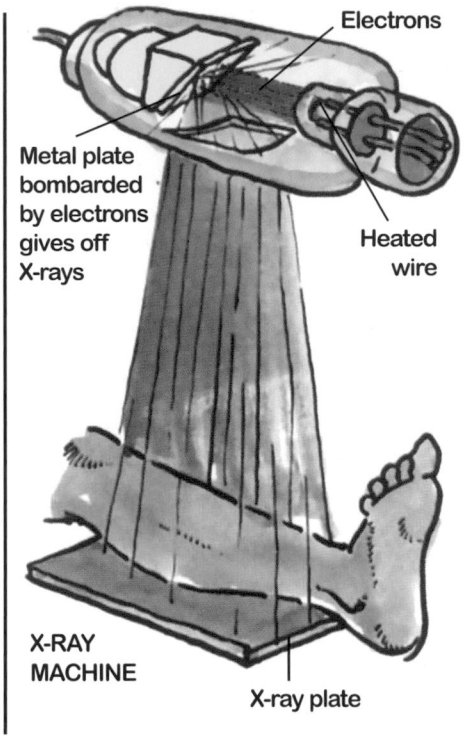

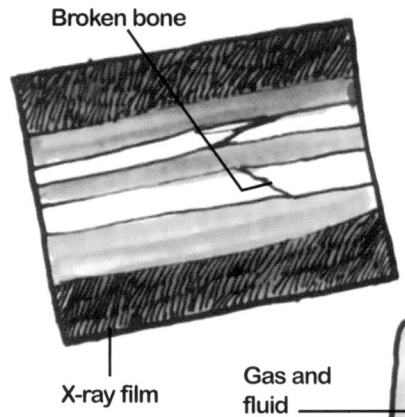

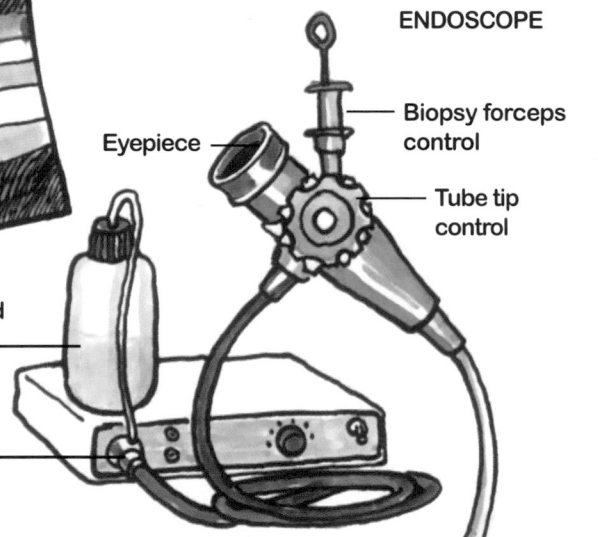

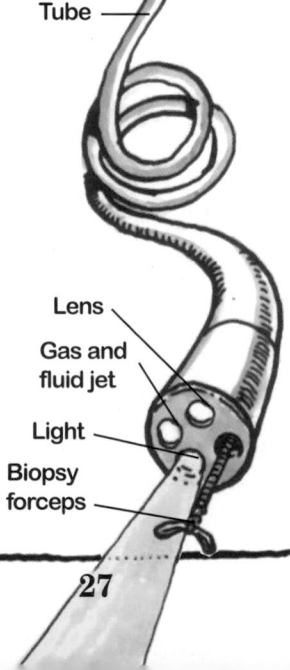

Whoops! Not a good idea

• Malaria is a serious illness spread by the bites of certain mosquitoes, which lay their eggs in water. Years ago, people thought malaria was spread by stale air (malaria means 'bad air'). So they put sweet-smelling flowers in pots of water by the bedside. The mosquitoes laid their eggs in the water, hatched out and bit the sleeping people, and the illness spread even faster!

• 'Ring-a-ring-a-roses, A pocket full of posies, A-tishoo, A-tishoo, All fall down.' A nice nursery rhyme? In fact, it could be about the Great Plague. People kept roses and other flowers, hoping the scent would keep the plague away. If they caught the plague, they sneezed, and soon many fell down dead. But modern experts say that story is not true. Shame!

THE ELECTRIC LIGHT

You are sitting quietly at home one evening, very interested in your school homework. Then 'pop', the light bulb goes out. Everything is dark. Before light bulbs, night was a twilight world of flickering camp fires, smoky candles, smelly oil lamps and hissing gas lights. Now we can turn night into day by flipping a light switch.

American inventor Thomas Edison came up with many bright ideas, like the phonograph (page 30). Brightest of all was the electric light bulb, in about 1880.

Thomas Edison

There were electric lights at the time. These were mostly arc lamps, where a non-stop electric spark jumped across a small gap between the ends of two rods. Arc lamps were glaring, unreliable and costly. Yet people gasped with wonder, because they were so bright.

White-hot glow

Edison thought that a cheaper, better electric light would become popular and make him lots of money. He was right. The key was to find the best substance for the glowing filament. He tested hundreds, from platinum wire to fibres in bamboo stems! His first successful filament, of specially treated cotton, glowed for 13½ hours.

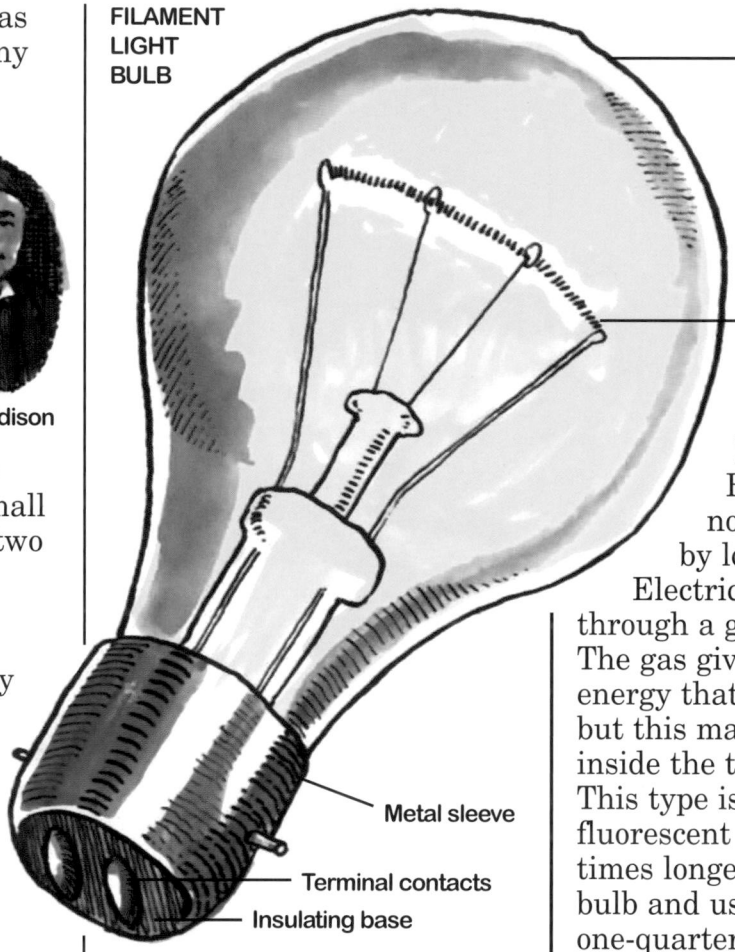

English chemist Joseph Swan had invented a similar light bulb. At first he and Edison argued, but this wasted money, so they joined forces. In 1882, US factories made 100,000 light bulbs. By 1900, production reached over 35 million. Darkness was banished. Evenings – and school homework – have never been the same since.

Low-energy light

Filament bulbs are now being replaced by low-energy ones. Electricity passes through a gas inside a tube. The gas gives out light energy that we cannot see, but this makes the coating inside the tube glow brightly. This type is known as the fluorescent light. It lasts 10 times longer than a filament bulb and uses less than one-quarter of the electricity.

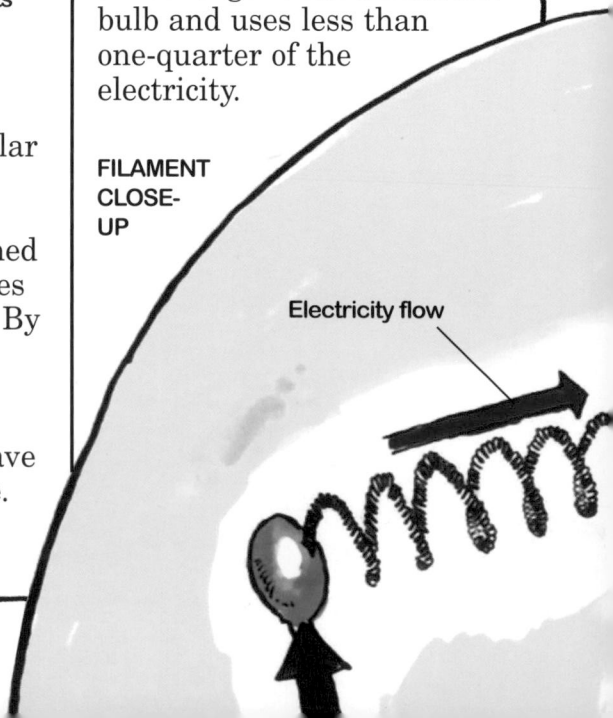

THE ELECTRIC MOTOR

Food blender. Washing machine. Spin dryer. Tumble dryer. Hair dryer. Electric fan. Central heating pump. Fridge compressor. Electric drill. Garden pond fountain. Electric mower. Vacuum cleaner. Computer disk drive. Starter motor on a car. Toy electric trains and cars. Real electric trains and cars. Make this list as long as you like. Electric motors are everywhere.

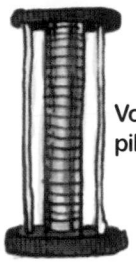

Volta's pile

In 1800, Italian professor Alessandro Volta made the first battery. It gave a steady flow of electric current. But what for? No one had invented a machine to use electricity.

In about 1820, English scientist Michael Faraday put a wire coil carrying an electric current near to a magnet. The magnet tried to move. He had the idea that electrical power could be converted into movement.

Michael Faraday

Faraday let a wire dangle near a magnet. When electricity flowed through the wire, it moved, and circled round and round the magnet. This was the principle of the electric motor.

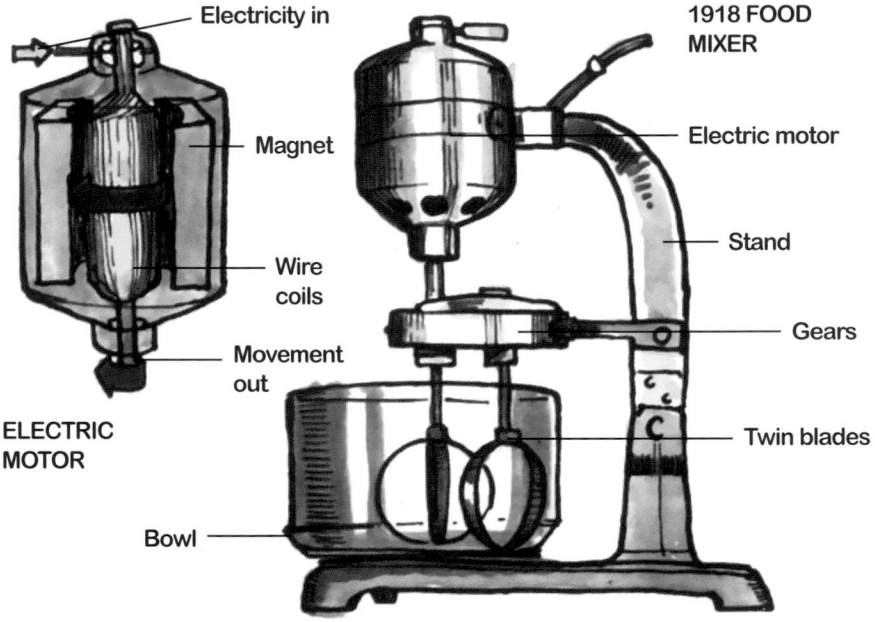

Drills and lathes

In the 1830s, inventors built practical electric motors. American engineer Thomas Davenport made a motor to turn a drill, and another for a lathe. But the motors were weak and they soon used up the battery power.

From the 1880s, electricity wires were installed in some factories, offices and homes. Electricity was 'on tap'. It could be used to power electric motors, which soon became smaller, faster and cheaper. Motorised food mixers and sewing machines were common in the 1930s. Look around your house today, count the electric motors, and imagine doing all their jobs by hand!

Whoops! Success and failure

• During the Apollo Moon landings of the early 1970s, astronauts drove about on the Moon in a Lunar Rover. It was powered by electric motors and had a top speed of 13 km/h (8 mph).

• The Sinclair C5 was a small single-seater 'car', powered by the type of electric motor used in washing machines. It came out in 1985, and was an instant flop.

THE PHONOGRAPH

'And this week's number one in the pop charts, with over a million sold, is *Fifty-Three-and-a-Half,* by Dave 'n' Steve!' The record charts, along with vinyl records, cassettes and compact discs, and the whole area of recorded music and speech, began with 'Mary had a little lamb.'

It's him again. In 1877 Thomas Edison had the idea of recording sound so it could be played back afterwards.

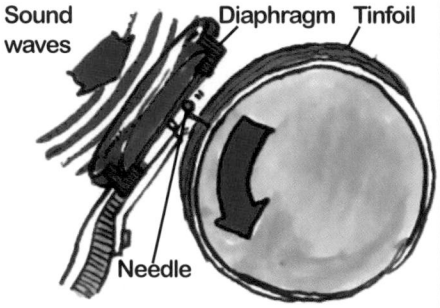

Edison designed a machine in which sound waves hit a thin, flat, metal sheet called a diaphragm. The waves made the diaphragm vibrate. The vibrations passed into a stylus or 'needle'. This pressed on a sheet of tinfoil, which was turning round on a cylinder. As the cylinder turned, the stylus pressed harder or softer for the different sounds, and made an up-and-down groove in the tinfoil. This was the recording.

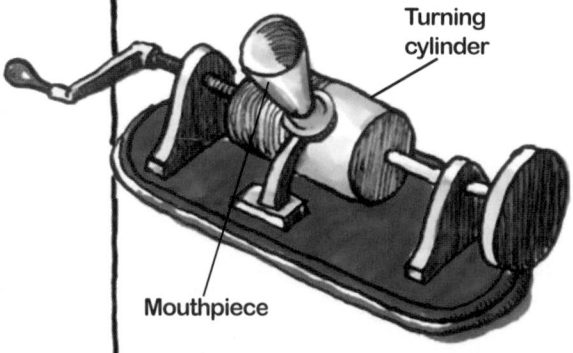

Groovy sounds

The recording in the tinfoil was changed back into sound waves by reversing the process. The cylinder turned, and the grooves made the stylus vibrate. These vibrations passed to the diaphragm, which shook the air around it, to make the original sounds.

The machine was called a phonograph. Edison spoke into it for a test recording: 'Mary had a little lamb.' It worked!

Other inventors saw that the phonograph could be used for music and entertainment. In 1885, they used a cylinder covered with wax instead of tinfoil. Lots of copies of one recording could be made by pouring hot wax into a mould, which was shaped like the cylinder with its groove.

Cylinder to disc

In 1887, Emile Berliner came up with a flat disc, instead of a cylinder. The stylus was in a wavy groove and vibrated from side to side as well as up and down as in Edison's version. Again, many discs could be made from one original.

Berliner did not want his version to be confused with Edison's phonograph, so he called it the Gram-o-Phone. He gradually improved the sound quality. Soon people were buying the first recordings of songs. The 'charts' had begun!

LPs to singles

Early record discs went round 78 times each minute, or 78 rpm (revolutions per minute). The discs were made of shellac. Vinyl records were introduced in 1946.

In 1948, the first successful long-playing records came out. They had much narrower grooves, went round at 33⅓ rpm, and lasted up to 30 minutes on each side.

Soon after, smaller vinyl discs came out. They usually had a single song on each side, they were seven inches across, and they went round at 45 rpm. They became known as 'singles' or '45s'. They began to sell in their millions and the chart competitions hotted up.

45s

Early 1950s tape recorder

Tape reel

Speaker

1992 Sony Walkman

Tapes big and small

In the 1950s, enthusiasts recorded sounds as patterns of tiny magnetic patches, on a long tape. The big tape reels were awkward to handle, and they took a long time to wind to and fro.

In the 1960s, the Philips company brought out much smaller magnetic tapes, in little plastic cases or 'case-ettes'. They were neat and easy to handle. You could buy them already recorded, or make your own recordings. The cassette had arrived.

Tape cassette

In the 1980s, compact discs began to take over. They had patterns of microscopic bumps and pits, detected by a laser beam.

If Edison could see all the ways we manipulate music today, he would be most amazed!

MP3s and iPods

Sounds have been stored in computer memories for many years. In the 1990s the MP3 file format became easily available. Like a CD, it records sounds in digital form, as strings of 0s and 1s, rather than as waves. With computer downloads, there is no physical evidence of an individual song at all.

iPod

Apple launched its iPod range of small digital players in 2001. Now cellphones (mobile phones) carry digital sounds too.

Horn

Needle

Turntable

Pits

Laser beam

Compact disc

GUNS AND GUNPOWDER

Bang! Crack! BOOM! The sound of gunfire echoes through the deserted streets, as freedom fighters battle with government troops ... Another war is about to change people's lives. Muskets to machine guns and cannon, in hands or on tanks, battleships and fighter planes, are still spitting death and destruction.

Gunpowder was the first explosive, invented in China about nine hundred years ago. It spread to the Middle East and Europe by the 1300s. Set alight by a spark or flame, gunpowder burns all at once, in a split second, with a cloud of smoke, an enormous blast and a huge BANG.

Wherever gunpowder went, people used its destructive powers for good and evil. One method was to put a barrel of gunpowder next to the thing you wanted to destroy, light a long fuse, and run. BOOM!

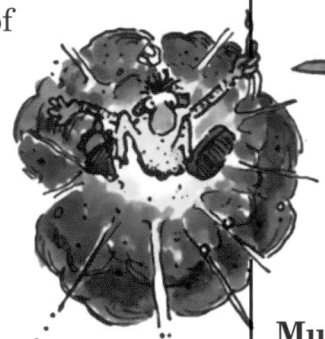

Matches and flints

The first guns were simple cannons, tubes of wood bound with iron rings. Tip gunpowder into the open end, followed by a tight-fitting stone or metal ball. Set light to the gunpowder through the small touch-hole at the closed end, and BANG.

During the 1400s, the matchlock was developed. It had a long metal barrel. Pull the trigger and a glowing rope hit the touch-hole, to set off the gunpowder. By the early 1600s a spark from a flint set off the gunpowder, in the flintlock.

These guns had wooden handles, or stocks. The stock let the firer aim properly, hold the hot metal barrel, and cope with the recoil or 'kick' of the explosion.

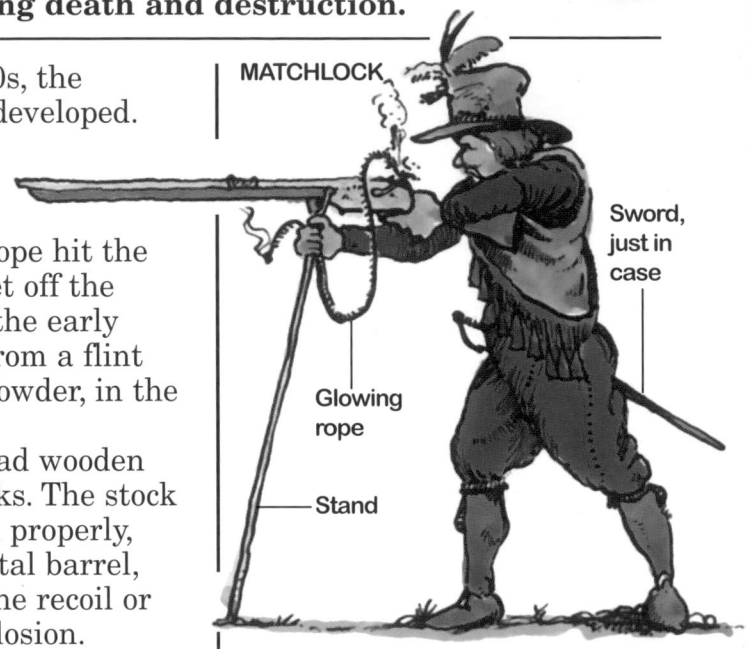

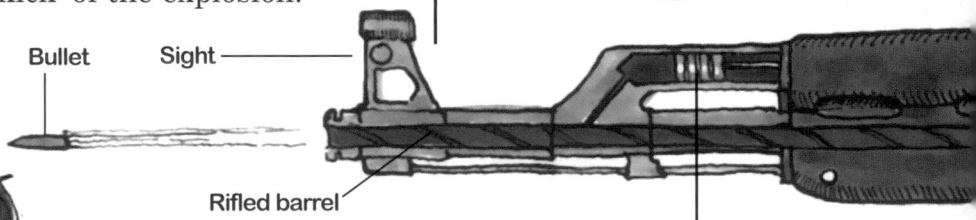

AK47 KALASHNIKOV SELECTIVE-FIRE RIFLE

Muzzles and breeches

Early guns were loaded by dropping the gunpowder and ball into the muzzle, the open end. This was slow and awkward, especially while the enemy was shooting back! Also, when gunpowder got wet, it did not work.

So percussion ignition and breech-loading guns were invented. Pull the trigger, and a hammer hits the percussion cap in the end of the cartridge, setting off a tiny explosion. This fires the main powder in the cartridge, which blasts the ball or bullet along the barrel. Cartridges were loaded through an opening at the back end, or breech, of the barrel. This basic system is still used today.

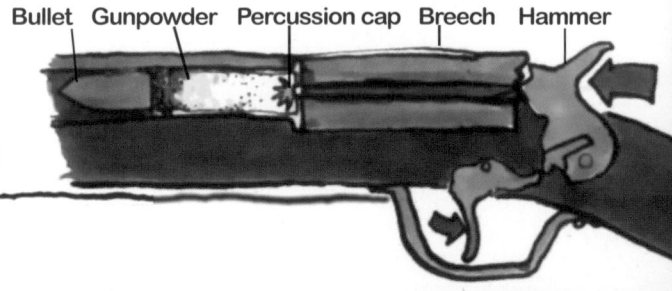

Rifles and revolvers

'Rifling' is a spiral groove along the inside of a gun barrel. It makes the bullet spin, so that it goes straighter to its target. After breech-loading arrived, most guns could be rifled, and they soon were.

Guns dominated America's Wild West. The legendary Winchester '73 repeater rifle was light enough to use on horseback. To speed up firing, small hand-guns were fitted with six-holed chambers that revolved around after each shot, to use the same barrel. They were revolvers or six-shooters. The most popular gun ever made was the Colt Single-Action Army Revolver, the 'Peacemaker'.

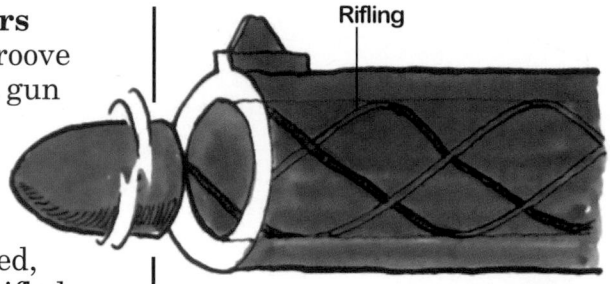

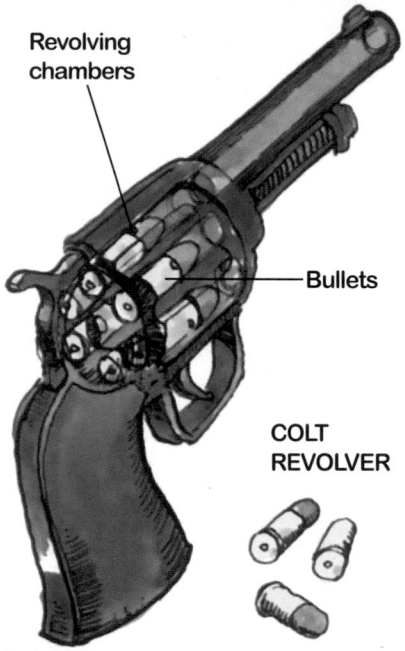

Penny for the Guy

• On 4 November 1605, Guy Fawkes prepared to blow up King James I of England and his Parliament. Fawkes was in a Catholic group that wanted to overthrow the Protestant king and his followers. He put barrels of gunpowder in the cellars, below where the king would sit the next day. But the gunpowder plot was discovered, and Fawkes was executed. We celebrate Guy Fawkes night on 5 November each year with gunpowder fireworks.

Mikhail Timofeyenich Kalashnikov

The soldier's friend

Today, the gun is still the soldier's basic weapon. One of the best is still the 1947 Kalashnikov AK47 automatic – fast-shooting, light, accurate, and devastating. Guns are also used for sport shooting, as collector's pieces, and to keep the law.

Explosives such as guncotton, dynamite and TNT have replaced gunpowder. But guns still play a major part in world affairs, from crime-busting to winning the revolution.

• Having a gun gives great power in some parts of the world, where 'war lords' rule by bullets rather than votes.

TELEPHONES AND MOBILES

'Can I order tickets for Friday by phone, please.'
'Did you hear about the great party last week?'
'Emergency, which service do you require?'
'Hello, is that you, Mum?'
A world without telephones would be a difficult place. We could only talk to people and pass on urgent messages when they were in front of us. And without our cellphones (mobiles), what would we do?

For thousands of years, communication was face-to-face. Only a few simple methods, like smoke signals from a fire, or the beating of drums, could be used to send messages quickly across long distances.

By the 1830s, battery power had arrived. People realised that if they had very long wires, they could send electric signals over great distances, using an on-off switch. The telegraph system was invented, and Samuel Morse came up with his dot-dash code.

The Morse Key

EARLY 1920s TELEPHONE

Mouthpiece

Varying current causes vibrations in diaphragm

Sound waves vibrate carbon granules to create a varying current

Earpiece stand

Earpiece

Numbered dial for calling through an automatic exchange

Magnet

BELL'S BOX TELEPHONE (1876)

Sound to electricity

Soon after the telegraph, inventors dreamed of making the electric signals copy the pattern of someone's voice.

Alexander Graham Bell was a doctor and speech teacher for deaf people. He knew about voices and sounds. In about 1876, in America, he made a simple machine that changed sounds to electrical signals. The signals flashed along a wire, almost a million times faster than sounds went through the air. A similar machine at the other end of the wire changed the signals back into sounds.

Alexander Graham Bell

Coast-to-coast phones

In 1877, Bell showed that his machine could send signals almost 30 kilometres, from Boston to Salem, USA. Within a few years, telephones were being installed in important buildings and in the homes of rich people.

At first, when you telephoned someone, all the connections were made by hand. Operators worked switches and plugs in the local exchange. The first automatic switches arrived in 1892. By 1915, Americans could phone coast-to-coast. Today, many phone systems use satellite links.

All the same signals

There are more than five billion phones in the world. We use them for texting, shopping, passing on messages, doing business, finding out information (such as the sports scores), and simply chatting.

When you talk into a telephone, it converts your voice to electrical signals. The phone lines can carry any similar type of small signals. So they can pass on signals from computers, radios, televisions, fax machines, laptops and many other gadgets.

How the telephone works

A telephone has two main parts. These are called the mouthpiece and the earpiece.

In the mouthpiece, sounds make a flat piece of metal vibrate. This squashes and stretches tiny bits of carbon in a container. Electricity goes through the carbon bits more easily when they are squashed, and less easily when they are stretched. So sounds are converted to very fast-changing electrical pulses or signals.

The signals go as radio waves or along wires to the earpiece of the other telephone. They pass through a coil of wire, called an electromagnet. The magnetism produced pulls on a nearby sheet of metal. The strength of the magnetism varies with the fast-changing signals, so the metal vibrates and makes sound waves.

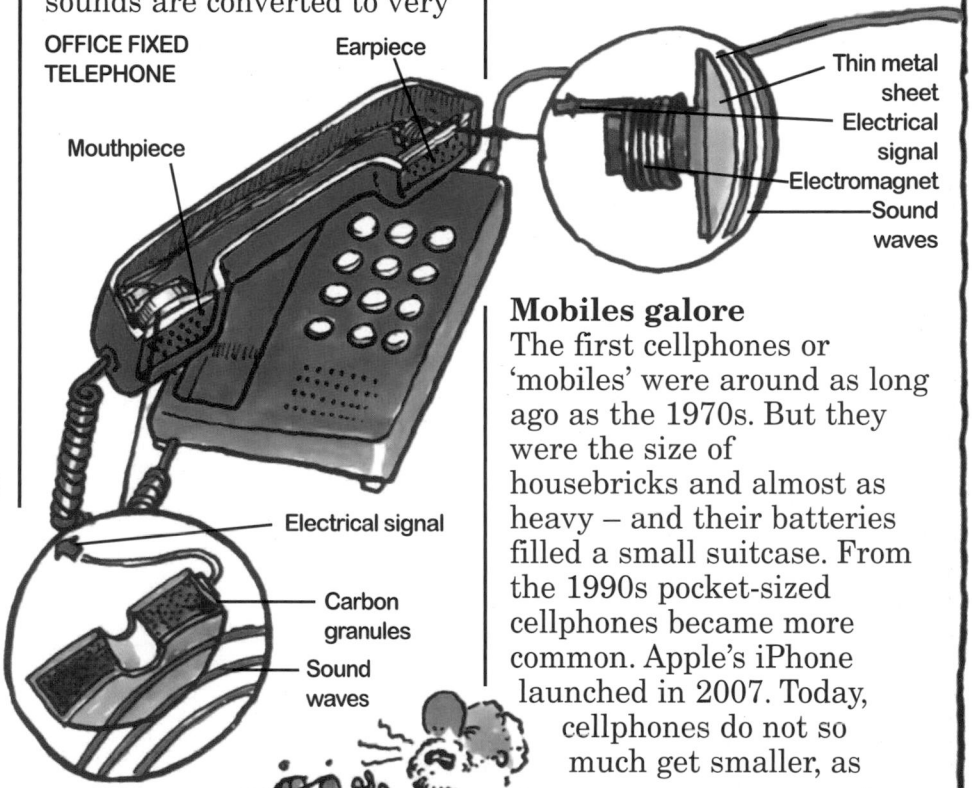

Mobiles galore

The first cellphones or 'mobiles' were around as long ago as the 1970s. But they were the size of housebricks and almost as heavy – and their batteries filled a small suitcase. From the 1990s pocket-sized cellphones became more common. Apple's iPhone launched in 2007. Today, cellphones do not so much get smaller, as more powerful. 'Smartphones' do music, video, texts, emails, Internet access, satnav and much more. Oh, and you can talk to people on them too!

RADIO

The air around us is full of waves. They carry messages and information on a vast range of matters, from weather forecasts to the latest news, from relaxing music to calls for help in emergencies. You cannot see the waves, or smell or feel them. But if you have a radio, you can hear what they have to say.

It began with numbers. In the 1860s, British scientist James Clerk Maxwell used mathematics to link light, heat, electricity and magnetism. He showed that invisible waves should be given off by an electric current that oscillated, or changed direction, many thousands of times each second.

Heinrich Hertz

In about 1887, German scientist Heinrich Hertz built an electrical gadget to show this. Another gadget at the other end of the room detected the waves and rang a bell. It was the first radio transmission, over a distance of 3 metres!

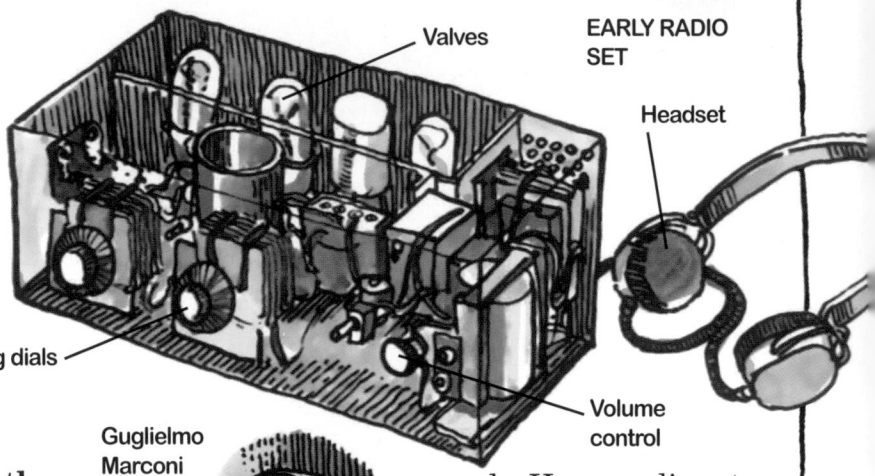

Guglielmo Marconi

Across the Atlantic

The invisible waves are called radio waves. By the 1890s, Guglielmo Marconi was trying to vary them, like the electricity in a telephone varied, to carry messages. With no wires between sender and receiver, it would be 'wireless'.

Marconi sent radio messages across the Channel between England and France. In 1901 he sent them much farther, across the Atlantic, from Cornwall to Newfoundland. Radio soon spanned the world.

The first radio messages were Morse code dots and dashes. Then radio receivers were designed to change the waves into electrical signals and feed these into a loudspeaker, to make sounds. Home radio sets became common from the 1920s.

Radio waves are used not only by radio sets, but also by televisions, mobile phones, satellites, navigation beacons, radio-control devices, radar, and dozens of other devices.

Someone had to be first

• In London in 1910, Dr Crippen killed his wife and escaped on a boat to America. Police sent a radio message to the boat in mid-ocean, and Crippen was captured. Radio had caught its first criminal!

• When Marconi died in 1937, the world's radio stations went silent for two minutes in his honour.

TELEVISION

Some people spend one-third of their lives asleep, one-third at work or school – and the other third watching television. Only fifty years ago, television was a new and wondrous invention. Try not to think of life without TV sets, computer screens and TV monitors of all kinds – it's too horrible!

After radio, scientists found ways to send pictures by radio waves, too.

John Logie Baird made a mechanical system in 1926. A wheel with a spiral pattern of holes whirled around. Each hole revealed a patch of light from the scene for a split-second. A light detector turned the patches into electrical signals, and a radio transmitter sent these as radio waves. The receiver was another whirling wheel, working in reverse.

John Logie Baird

TV milestones

Baird's system was used for a short while, but it had mechanical problems. The electronic TV system as we know it today was devised by Vladimir Zworykin, in America in the 1920s.

In 1936, a regular TV service (in black and white) started in London. A regular colour TV service began in America in 1951, and came to Britain in 1967.

How flatscreen TVs work

Most TV sets are now flatscreens rather than the old 'fatscreens'. Typical home sets use LCs, liquid crystals. These crystal-like items change the way they transmit light by twisting or polarising their structure, horizontal or vertical, to let similarly polarised light through, and blocking light polarised in the other direction. The crystals build up the picture from tiny units called pixels or 'picture elements'. Each pixel has red, green and blue colours to make the full range of other colours, including white when all three colours shine at once.

I'm a star!

• Baird tried his first mechanical TV in his attic. He rushed out and asked a passing boy to help. Back in the attic, Baird sent pictures of the face of the surprised boy – the first TV star.

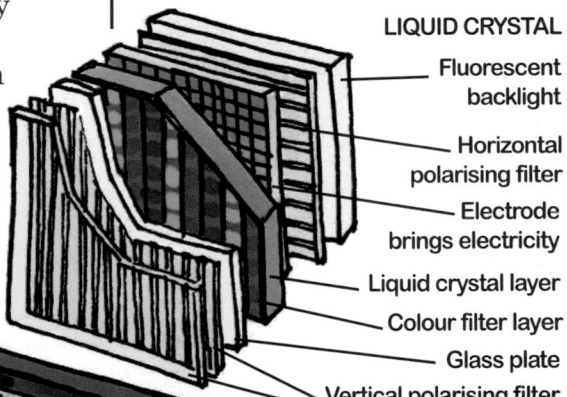

3D TV
There are several ways to produce a three-dimensional screen effect. In one system the front of the screen is covered with transparent ridges called lenticular lenses. These angle different parts of the image to the left and right eyes.

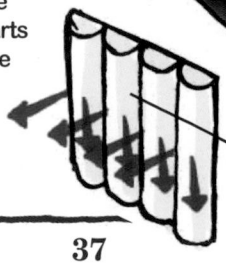

THE STEAM ENGINE

Aaah, the Golden Age of Steam. Locomotives puffing across the countryside, and steam-powered machines clanking away on farms and in factories. Watt happened to steam engines? They were noisy, dirty and inefficient, that's watt! So they aren't used much today. But for a time, steam power was the best invention of the Industrial Revolution – which changed our world forever.

Hero, of Ancient Greece, made a simple engine using steam (page 44). But the modern Age of Steam began with Thomas Savery, an English military engineer, in about 1698.

Tin was a valuable metal. But the tin mines in Cornwall were often flooded by water seeping through the rocks. Savery's engine pumped out the water.

A fire heated water in a boiler, to give off steam. This passed into a large iron vessel, the condenser. Water sprayed over the outside, and the steam inside cooled and condensed into water. This left a vacuum, which sucked water up a pipe from the mine. More steam pushed the water away along another pipe.

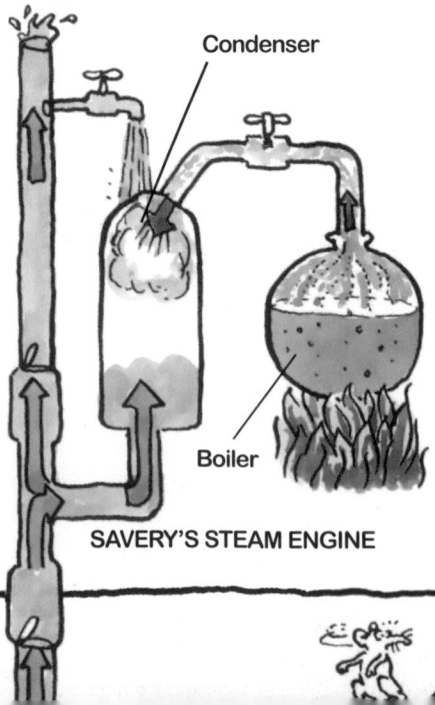

SAVERY'S STEAM ENGINE

Another Thomas

An English ironmonger, Thomas Newcomen, made the next advance in 1712. His engines pumped water from coal mines near Birmingham.

Newcomen's steam engine

The Newcomen version had a piston inside a cylinder. Steam was let into the bottom of the cylinder as the piston moved up. Then water sprayed onto the cylinder and condensed the steam, making a vacuum which sucked the piston down. The piston's up-and-down movements rocked a crossbeam that worked a water pump.

Guess Watt's next ...

The father of steam

Yes, it's famous Scottish engineer, James Watt. He did not invent the steam engine, but by the 1780s he had made several great improvements.

One was a separate condenser, to change the steam back into water. This meant the main cylinder did not have to heat up and cool down all the time, which wasted energy. Another improvement was squirting steam into one side of the cylinder, to push the piston one way, then squirting it into the other side, to push the piston back. Yet another Watt advance was to change the up-and-down motion of a piston into the round-and-round motion of a wheel, using a connecting rod. Steam power had arrived!

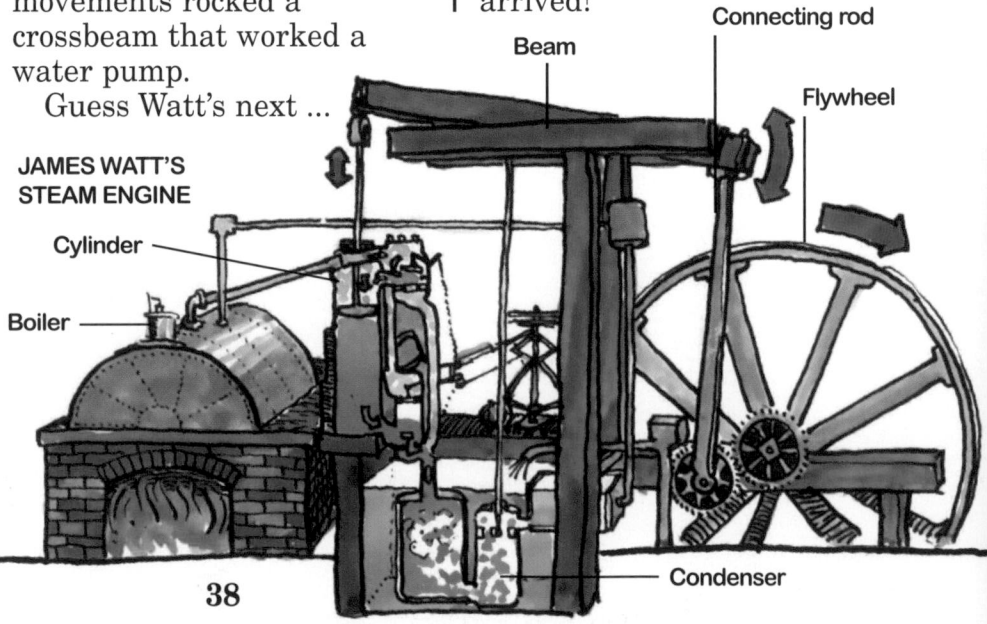

JAMES WATT'S STEAM ENGINE

The coming of the railways

Richard Trevithick was a mine engineer in Cornwall. Many mines at the time had iron rails, for hauling wagons. Trevithick put railway wheels on a Watt-type steam engine and made the first locomotive, for mine work, in 1804.

Steam locomotives were soon chuffing through the countryside. The first steam passenger railway opened in 1825 between Stockton and Darlington, in northern England. Its locomotive *Locomotion* No. 1 was designed by George Stephenson. In 1829, Stephenson's better *Rocket* pulled 20-tonne wagons at 40 km/h (25 mph).

Trevithick's steam engine

Many uses for steam

Within twenty years, almost every European country had a railway network. Steam engines were also powering cotton mills, iron foundries and a host of other machines.

New forms of transport appeared: paddle- and screw-driven steamships, steam-powered traction engines and tractors, and steaming cars!

Steam engines also turned the generators for Thomas Edison in 1882, at New York's first electricity-generating power station.

Piston-power steam engines are rare today. But steam still generates most of our electricity, by whirling the blades of steam turbines.

Whoops! Not a good idea

• Nicolas Cugnot, a French soldier, built a three-wheeled steam-driven carriage in 1769. It was supposed to pull heavy cannons, but it went out of control and crashed. Cugnot's commanders decided to stick with horses.

CUGNOT'S CARRIAGE

• Another Frenchman, Clément Ader, made a steam-powered aeroplane in 1890. But it was far too heavy and never took off.

STEPHENSON'S *ROCKET*

Stack

Boiler

Drive wheel

Piston

Driver

THE INTERNAL COMBUSTION ENGINE

Walk along the street. Niaooww – a motorbike races past. Vrroom – a sports car chases it. Brrmm, a family saloon cruises by, followed by the ear-shattering Rrooaar of a juggernaut truck, and a taxi Dg-dg-dg. They are all powered by IC engines, an essential part of today's living.

What's an internal combustion or IC engine? You guessed: an engine that combusts or burns fuel inside it. The two main kinds are petrol (gasoline) and diesel. They vary from thumb-sized engines in model planes, to house-sized diesel engines in ships and trains.

IC engines can power motorbikes, cars, trucks, planes, locomotives, tractors, boats, home electricity generators, cement mixers, lawn-mowers, hedge-cutters and many more. Without their phutts, vrooms and brrmms, our world would be quieter and less polluted. It'd also be much slower, and harder work – no cars, and mowing the lawn by muscle power!

How the IC engine works

Like steam engines, IC engines have pistons, cylinders and cranks. These change to-and-fro oscillating motion into more useful round-and-round rotary motion. When the fuel burns in the engine, it creates tremendous pressure and pushes a piston along a cylinder.

The average petrol engine is four-stroke, meaning the piston makes four strokes – two up, two down – for each complete cycle. It has four pistons and cylinders. Each fires at a different time, for overall smooth running.

SINGLE CYLINDER 4-STROKE ENGINE

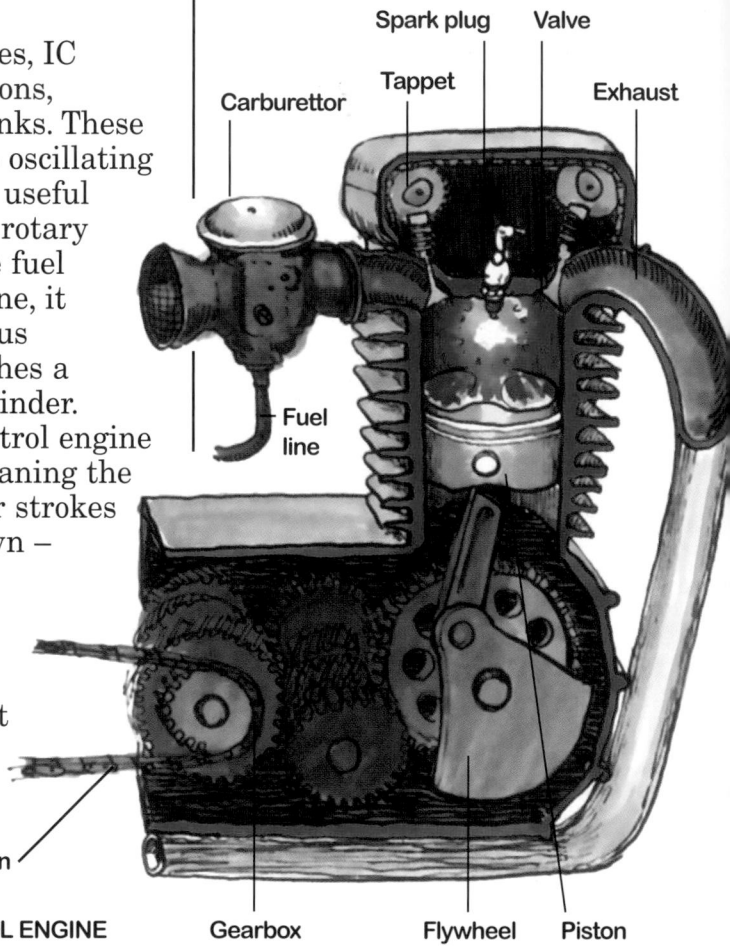

THE 4-STROKE PETROL ENGINE

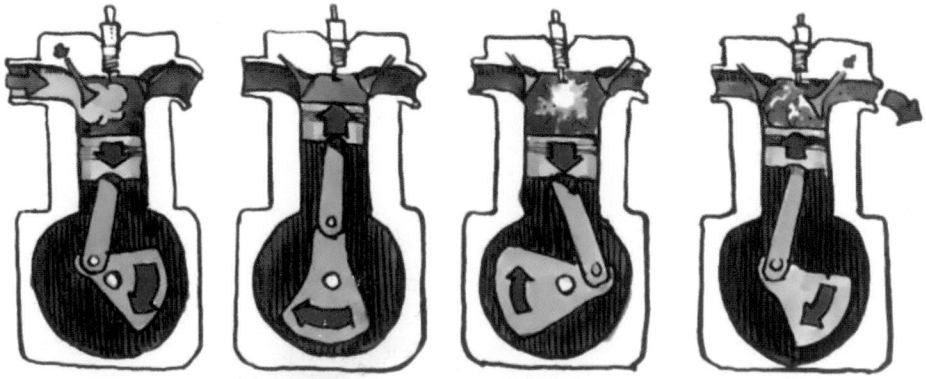

Stroke 1
Fuel/air mixture drawn in

Stroke 2
Fuel/air mixture compressed

Stroke 3
Spark plug ignites fuel/air mixture

Stroke 4
Exhaust gases pushed out

Diesel engine

This has no spark plugs. It compresses the air much more than a petrol engine, which makes it so hot that when the fuel is sprayed in, it explodes. Diesel engines are usually more reliable and economical than petrol engines, but bigger, heavier and noisier.

THE FOUR-STROKE DIESEL ENGINE

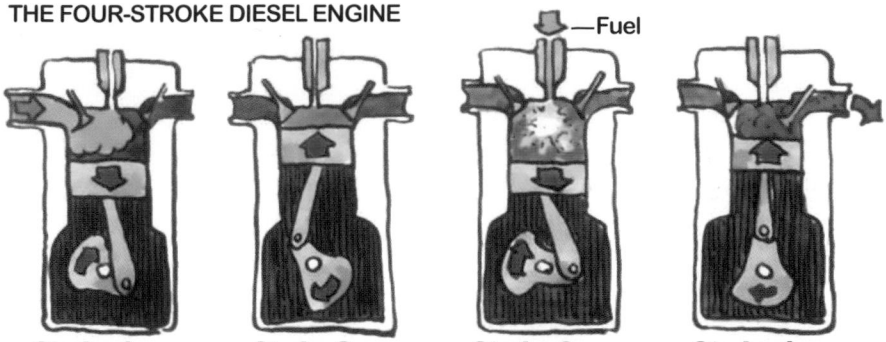

Stroke 1 Air drawn in

Stroke 2 Air compressed

Stroke 3 Diesel injected and explodes

Stroke 4 Exhaust gases pushed out

Cars for everyone

The first mass-produced cars with IC engines were Model T Fords, made in the USA from 1908. They freed people from horses and trains and legs, and let them motor when and where they wanted. They signaled a vast change in everyday life.

Cars were already around. The first modern-style car was the Mercedes, developed by the German engineer Gottlieb Daimler in 1900. He had already invented the first lightweight, high-speed, IC petrol engine in 1883. Soon afterwards he fitted one to a bicycle, making the first motorbike.

Also in the 1880s, another German engineer named Karl Benz built his Motorwagen. It was a 14 km/h (9 mph) three-wheeler, powered by a petrol-fuelled IC engine – the start of modern motoring.

Model T Ford

The first motorbike

It was a busy time. In 1892 yet another engineer in Germany, Rudolf Diesel, converted a steam engine and invented the engine named after him. It took him over five years to make a successful version.

Rudolf Diesel and his first diesel engine

From gas power to hybrids

Cars were not the earliest use for IC engines. The first practical IC engines ran on piped gas, and went nowhere. They were invented by German engineer Nikolaus Otto in 1876, and they replaced steam engines in some factories.

In modern hybrid cars, an IC engine and an electric motor share the work. The IC engine can charge the electric batteries when they run down.

The first car, built by Karl Benz in 1885

Seemed like a good idea at the time

• In the 1600s, Dutch scientist Christiaan Huygens thought about an IC engine using gunpowder-power! His idea came from the cannon, which is like a 'one-stroke' IC engine. The ball is the piston, the barrel is the cylinder. The gunpowder explodes and pushes the piston along the cylinder. If the gunpowder could be quickly renewed and fired again ... well, it's just as well it couldn't!

THE AEROPLANE

If you had lots of money, where would you go for a three-week holiday? A tropical island or a wildlife-packed rainforest? Without an aeroplane, it would take you three weeks just to get there! Aeroplanes made the world smaller. People travel ten times faster than in a car, boat or train.

For centuries, flying was a dream. Brave men built bird-like wings and tried to flap from cliffs, only to crash to their doom. Scientific thinkers realised the human body was not designed for flight. It needed help.

Lighter than air

The first person to get airborne was Frenchman Jean Pilatre de Rozier. In 1783, he took off in a cloth-and-parchment balloon built by brothers Joseph and Jacques Montgolfier. The balloon was tied to a rope, and it rose because it had smoky hot air (from a fire) inside.

A few weeks later, de Rozier and the Marquis d'Arlandes floated freely over Paris in a bigger balloon. But this was not a true, controlled flight. Balloons simply drift with the wind.

Gliding

Gliding is not very controlled either. Gliders cannot stay up for a long time, but they helped the early study of aircraft design and control.

German engineer Otto Lilienthal greatly improved glider design. From 1891 he built over 20 types of glider, and he made over 2,000 flights. But he crash-landed and died in 1896.

Otto Lilienthal

Cloth covering

Wooden frame

Orville Wright

Lightweight engine powers two pusher propellers

Wilbur Wright

WRIGHT *FLYER* 1

The first aeroplane

Lilienthal's death greatly affected American brothers Wilbur and Orville Wright. For seven years, these bicycle engineers studied gliders and made model planes. They realised the steam engines and early petrol engines of the time were too heavy for a plane. They designed their own lightweight version.

The Wrights built the first real aeroplane, the *Flyer*. Orville flew it on a windy beach near Kitty Hawk, North Carolina, USA, on 17 December 1903. His first trip lasted just 12 seconds and covered 37 metres, but the Age of the Aeroplane had begun.

The Wrights' lightweight four-cylinder engine

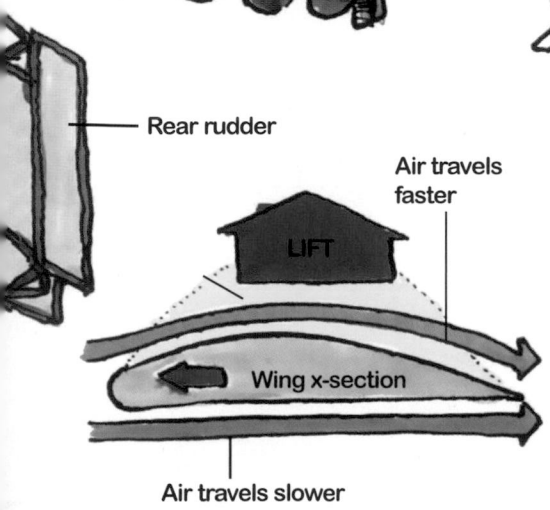

Air travel

At first, planes were a curiosity. They put on shows for open-mouthed crowds. At the start of World War One in 1914, pilots checked enemy troop positions and shot each other with pistols.

The first international passenger services began weekly in 1919, between Paris and Brussels. The first flight from London to Paris was by Air Travel and Transport Limited. It carried just one passenger!

Aeroplanes began to affect everyday life in the 1920s. Rich and important people could fly across a continent or ocean in a few hours. Air mail meant a letter reached the other side of the world in a few days, not weeks.

Today many people have a pilot's licence and fly for fun. Planes carry cargoes and passengers to every part of the globe. A world without aeroplanes would be a much bigger place.

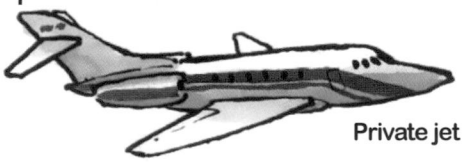

Private jet

How the wing works

An aeroplane wing is more curved on top than underneath. As it moves along, air has to rush faster over the top. This makes the air pressure lower on top, and higher below. It creates lift, and the wing gets 'pushed' upwards.

Whoops! Better luck next time

• An early air casualty was the monk Eilmer, of Malmesbury Abbey, England. Legend says that in about 1000 AD he jumped from the abbey tower with small wings strapped to his arms. He broke both legs!

• American scientist Samuel Langley test-flew his aeroplane, Aerodrome, a few weeks before the Wrights. It took off from a boat in the Potomac River – and crashed. After repairs, it crashed again. The newspapers enjoyed the failure. This is why, at first, people thought the Wright flight was a joke.

• Horatio Phillips' Multiplane had 20 thin wings, like a flying venetian blind! It made a few short flights in 1907, but then broke in half.

THE JET ENGINE

In the 1950s, jet airliners took to the skies. Air travel was becoming more common, and the speedier jets shrunk the world further. People could travel from England to Australia in less than two days. Meanwhile, countries raced to get the fastest jet-powered fighters and bombers. Without jets, war just wouldn't be the same!

A jet engine creates hot gases inside it, by burning its fuel in a sort of non-stop explosion. The gases blast out the back, and push the engine forwards. Since the 1950s, jets have taken over from propellers on most types of aeroplanes.

The first 'jet'?
Around 1,900 years ago in Ancient Greece, Hero made a simple type of jet engine. His hollow metal ball could spin on swivels. He heated water in the ball. Steam rushed out of two angled nozzles, and made the ball turn.

In the 19th Century, several people tried to invent jets. The idea was simple, but no metals could stand the enormous heat. In the late 1930s, World War Two loomed. It gave aircraft research a great push.

Hero's steam engine

The war of the jets
From 1930, English engineer Frank Whittle worked on jet engines. But the British government was not interested. Whittle had to work in an old shed, at the Royal Air Force base at Farnborough, Hampshire.

In 1937 Whittle test-fired his first jet engine, WU1, which was bolted on to his laboratory bench!

Frank Whittle

Gloster Meteor

In Germany, Hans von Ohain and Ernst Heinkel worked on similar designs. On 23 August 1939, a Heinkel He178 became the first jet plane to fly.

It was war, and advances came quickly. The first jet fighter, the German He280, took off in April 1941. Britain's answer, the Gloster Meteor, was the first jet fighter in action.

The first jet-to-jet combat was between US Sabres and Soviet MiG-15s in the Korean War, 1950.

Exhaust

Turbojet engine

USAF

The first German jets in action were Me262s, in September 1944. Pilots of the US 8th Air Force were amazed that these enemy planes had no propellers!

Me262

Peaceful uses

Jet planes came too late to have much effect on World War Two. But July 1949 saw the world's first jet airliner, Britain's de Havilland Comet. The US Boeing 707 began carrying passengers in 1958. The Airbus A380 'Super Jumbo' went into service in 2007.

Jets to the rescue

The speed of a jet plane can whisk politicians across the world, take the sick and injured to hospital, and carry emergency foods and medicines. Cargo jets bring exotic foods from faraway places before they go rotten! Millions of holidaymakers fly in passenger jets to warm, sunny places. A type of jet engine, the jet turbine, provides the power for another essential machine, the helicopter. The jet engine shapes our modern life in many such ways.

Westland Sea King helicopter

de Havilland Comet

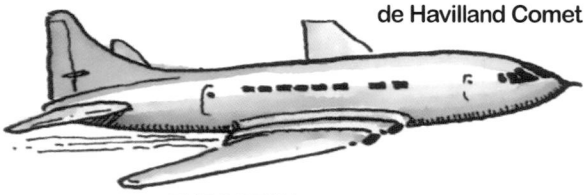

TURBOJET

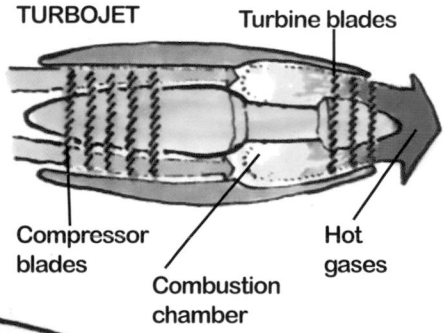

TURBOFAN

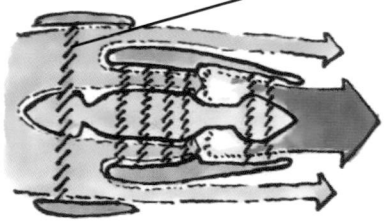

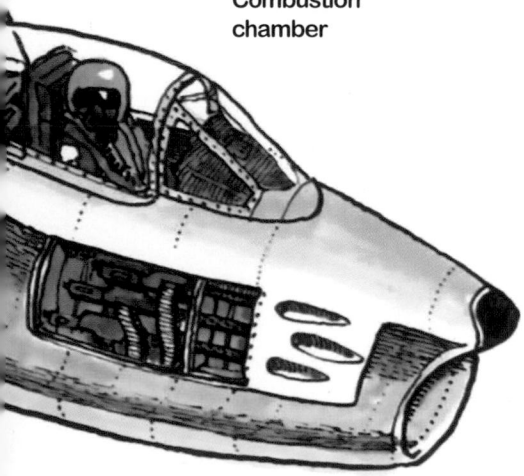

How jet engines work

A turbojet has fan-shaped compressor blades, to squash the incoming air before it burns the fuel. As the hot gases roar from the back, they turn turbine blades which work the compressors.

A turbofan has an extra-big fan at the front, which blows air around the sides of the main engine. It uses less fuel and is quieter than the turbojet. Most passenger jets have turbofans.

Jet record-breakers

• The fastest jetliner, Concorde, cruised at 2,330 km/h (1,450 mph). Because of the time change, you would leave London and then arrive in New York before you took off!

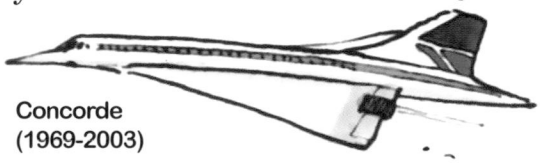

Concorde (1969-2003)

• The official air speed record is held by the US Lockheed SR71A 'Blackbird'. In 1976 it flew at 3,530 km/h (2,193 mph).

Blackbird

• The world's fastest car is the jet-powered Thrust SSC. In 1997 English pilot Andy Green drove it across America's Black Rock desert at 1,228 km/h (763 mph).

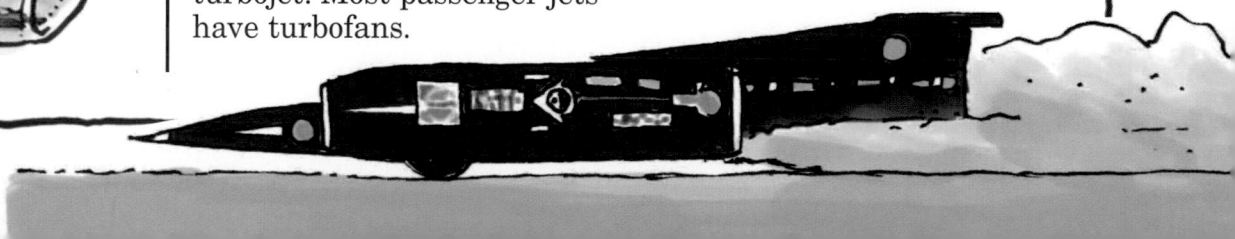

THE SPACE ROCKET

Space rockets themselves may not have changed the world, but their launch cargoes certainly have. Imagine life without satellites (page 48)! Orbiting telescopes see farther into space than telescopes on the ground, helping to unlock the secrets of the Universe. And space research has given us many spin-off products, such as the non-stick frying pan!

The Space Age began in 1957, when a Soviet A rocket launched the world's first satellite, Sputnik 1. But rocket research had been going on for many years before this.

Sputnik 1

The 'father of space flight' was Konstantin Tsiolkovsky, a Russian schoolteacher. In 1903 he wrote a book showing how a rocket could work, but he did no experiments.

The first rocket

In 1926 Robert Goddard, an American engineer, launched the world's first real rocket at Auburn, Massachusetts, USA. It used petrol and liquid oxygen and went up only 12 metres, just higher than an average house. But it was a start!

Goddard and rocket

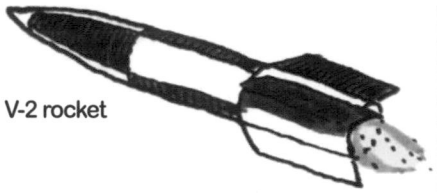

Goddard designed bigger, faster rockets that flew two kilometres high. Werner von Braun and his engineers in Germany did the same. Late in World War Two, German V-2 rocket-missiles bombed targets over 300 kilometres away.

A1 VOSTOK ROCKET

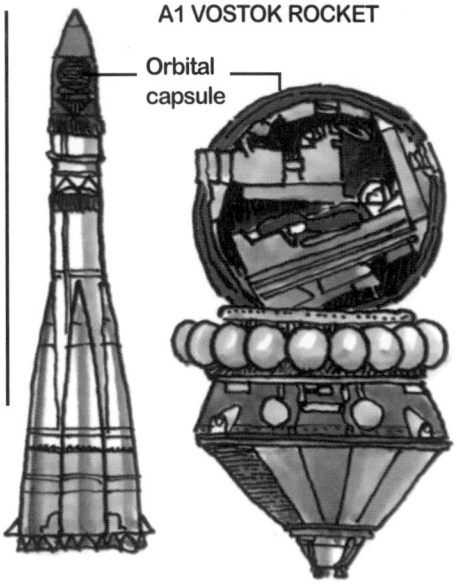

SATURN V ROCKET

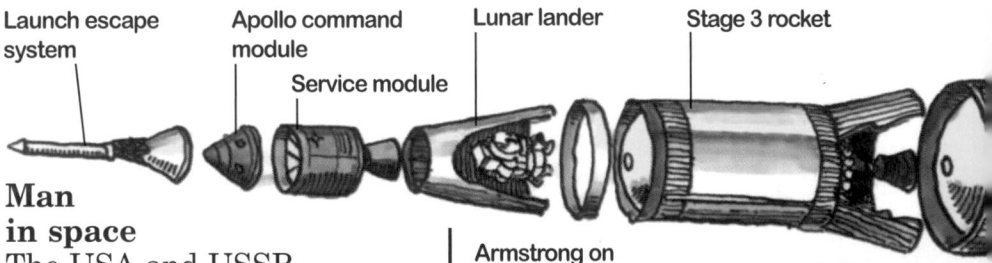

Man in space

The USA and USSR developed rockets for their long-range missiles. In the 1950s, these were powerful enough to fly 100 kilometres (62 miles) high, into space. To escape the Earth's gravity and float in space, a rocket must reach a speed of 40,000 km/h (25,000 mph).

The first spaceman was a Russian, Yuri Gagarin. In 1961 he took off in his Vostok spacecraft, on top of a Soviet A-1 rocket. First on the Moon were Americans Neil Armstrong and Edwin Aldrin. In 1969 they took off in their Apollo mooncraft, on top of a Saturn V rocket.

Armstrong on the Moon

Most space rockets, like the modern European Ariane, burned up after launch and became useless. In 1981 the USA flew a new kind of re-useable craft, the Space Shuttle. It glided back to Earth from space, to be used again.

Space spin-offs

Nowadays, rockets take off almost weekly. They carry satellites, space stations, experiments, deep-space probes and secret military equipment. Space research helps scientists to understand the human body, and to improve all kinds of delicate processes, such as making drugs and electronic circuits.

Over the years, space research has also come up with many 'spin-offs'. These ranged from better computers, to non-stick coatings on pans, silvery 'space blankets' used by mountaineers and exhausted runners, 'sticky spiders' that roll down a window, and new kinds of even stronger spider silk.

US SPACE SHUTTLE (1981–2011)

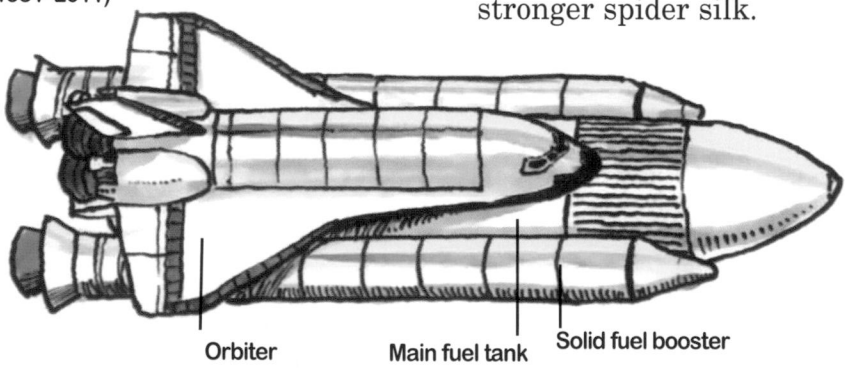

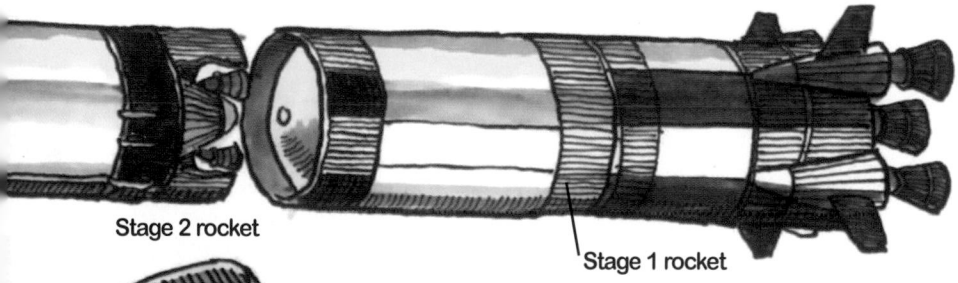

Whoops! Better luck next time

• The Apollo 13 Moon mission was in April 1970. Two days after take-off, an oxygen tank exploded and damaged the spacecraft. The astronauts reached the Moon, but could not land. They boosted straight back to Earth, returning safely four days later. Unlucky 13!

• In 1990 the US Navy test-fired a rocket-powered Trident missile, from a submarine under the ocean. The 32-tonne missile left the sub, reached the surface – then went out of control, spun round crazily, and crashed into the sea. Back to the drawing board!

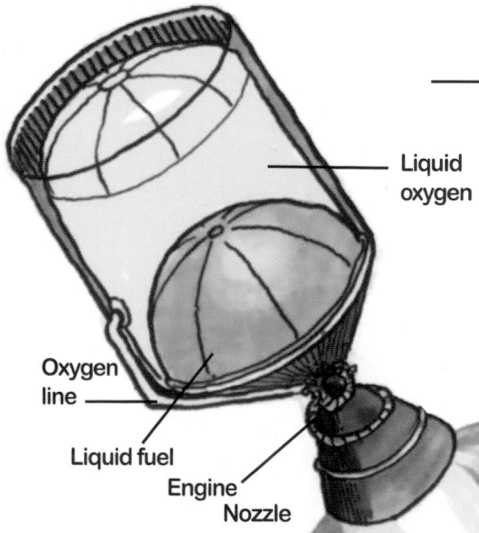

How a rocket works

At launch, the Space Shuttle had five rocket engines. They work like jet engines (page 44), burning fuel to create a blast of hot gases. A space rocket has its own supply of oxygen, called oxidiser. This is because fuel needs oxygen to burn, and there is no oxygen (nor much else) in space.

The Shuttle's two solid-fuel booster rockets fell off about two minutes after launch. The huge tank held fuel for its three liquid-fuel rocket engines. The tank fell off seven minutes later. In space, the Shuttle had enough fuel on board to fire its own engines and glide back to Earth.

THE SATELLITE

'And now, direct by satellite, we go live to the greatest music concert in history!' Our hi-tech world would end at once without space satellites. Global TV and radio, weather maps, Internet and telephone calls, ship and aeroplane navigation, spying on secret military projects, who's burning the tropical forests – satellites are vital to all these, and many more.

On 4 October 1957, the Soviet Union launched a rocket containing a shiny metal ball, 58 centimetres across, which held a small radio transmitter. It was the first satellite, Sputnik 1.

For three months it sent out a weak 'bleep-bleep' to radio stations on the ground. Then it fell to Earth and burned up.

Satellites galore

A satellite is anything that orbits, or goes round, something else. The Earth is a satellite, orbiting the Sun. But when people talk of a 'satellite', they usually mean something as big as a small truck, stuffed with electronics, bristling with radio dishes, solar panels and cameras, which a space rocket launches into orbit around the Earth.

Communications

Communications satellites, or comsats, receive radio signals from one part of the Earth and beam them down to a wider area, or to another region. The signals may be TV or radio programmes, telephone calls, computer and Internet information, or pathfinding signals from ships, submarines or aeroplanes.

One of the first successful satellites was Intelsat 1, also known as 'Early Bird'. It rocketed into space in 1965, and lasted four years. It could receive and send 240 telephone calls at the same time.

A modern comsat can handle more than a million telephone calls and hundreds of TV channels. It weighs two-plus tonnes, contains over 70,000 parts, and is powered by vast sunlight-capturing solar panels.

OLYMPUS series satellites were launched from 1989.

Early Bird

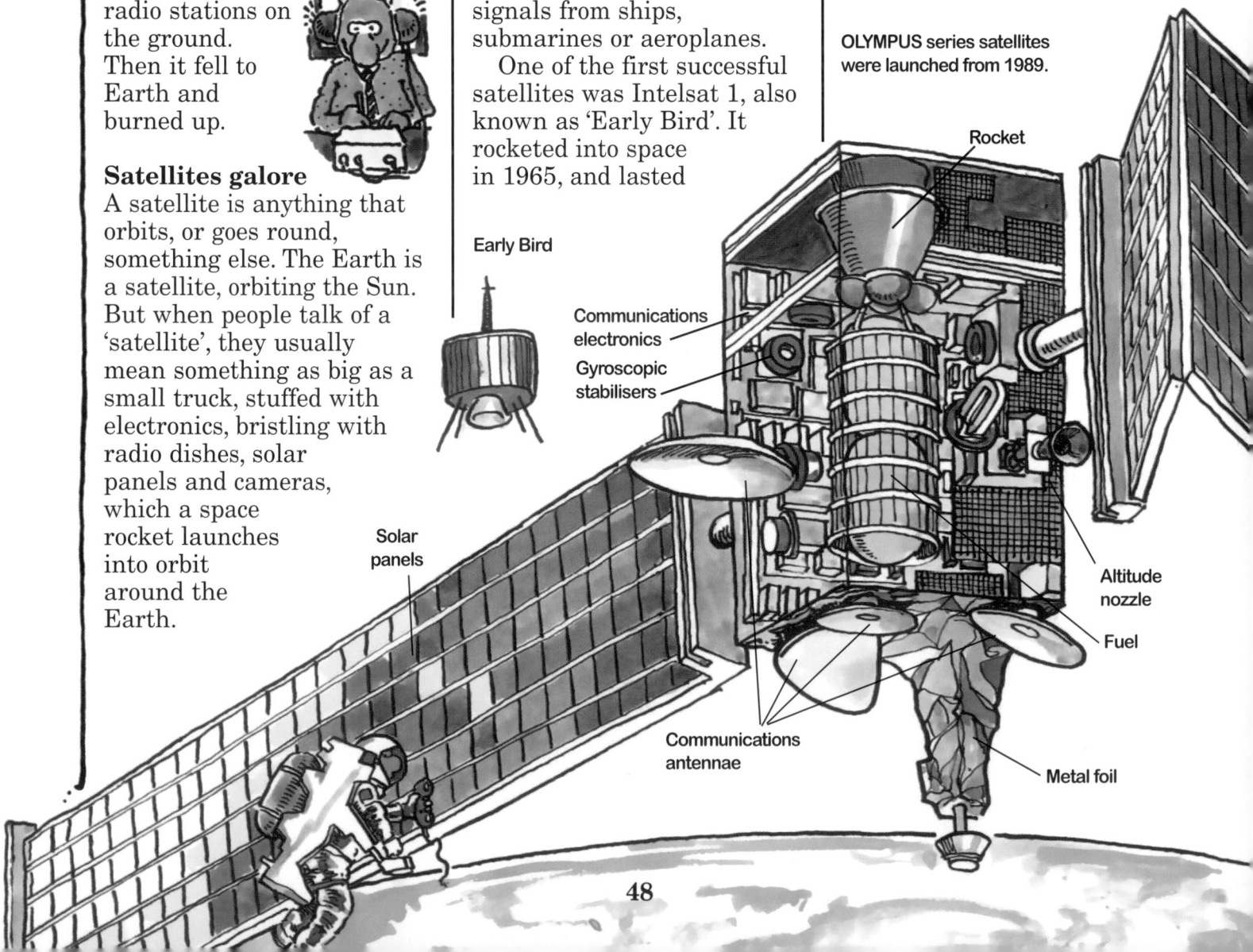

Research

Dozens of satellites are used for scientific research. Some look down on the Earth, taking special close-up or heat-pattern photographs, and pictures of clouds and weather. Others look deep into space. They get a much clearer view than they would from down on the surface. They detect light rays, radio waves, X-rays and many other kinds of rays and waves.

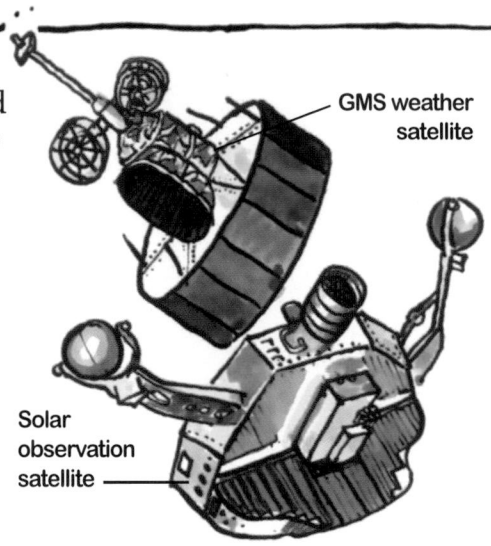

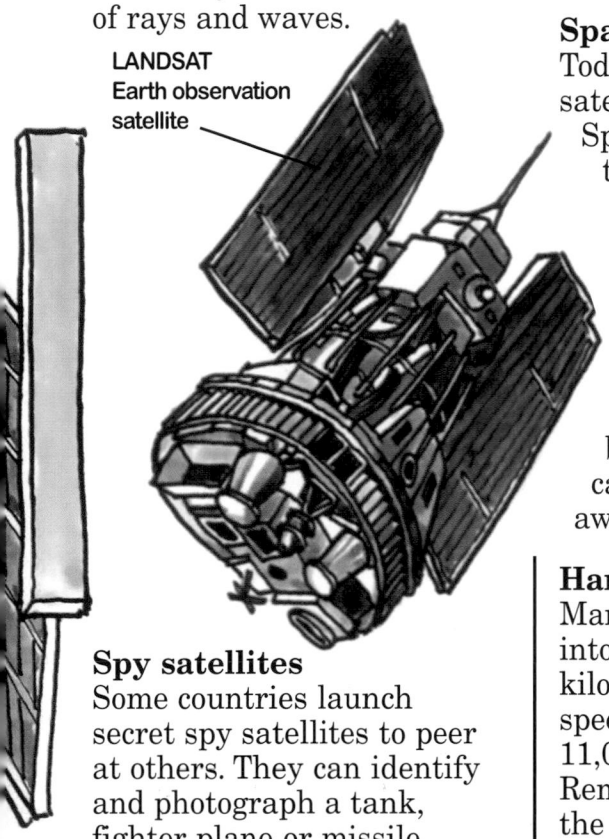

Space is getting crowded

Today, there are hundreds of satellites orbiting Earth. Space is vast, and there is only a tiny chance that one might crash into another. Even so, when a satellite is planned, the international space organisation must be told. Then the satellite can orbit well away from others.

The ones that nearly got away

- In 1984, the crew of the Space Shuttle mended a satellite called Solar Max as it orbited high above the Earth.
- On another mission, they repaired Leasat 3.
- The Shuttle also brought back two satellites, Palapa B2 and Westar 6, to Earth for repairs. At millions of pounds each, a broken satellite is an expensive piece of space junk!

Spy satellites

Some countries launch secret spy satellites to peer at others. They can identify and photograph a tank, fighter plane or missile launcher on the ground, from more than 100 kilometres up in space.

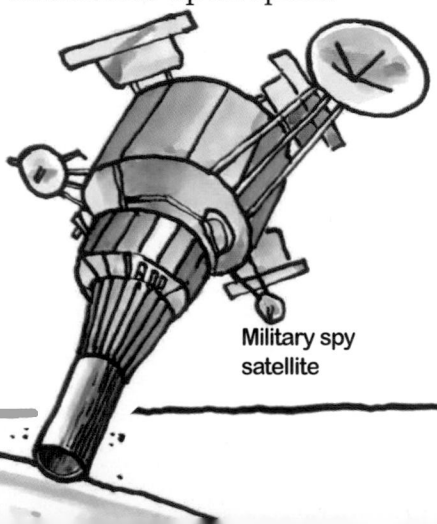

Hanging in the sky

Many comsats are launched into an orbit 36,000 kilometres high, where they speed through space at 11,000 kilometres per hour. Remember that, far below, the Earth spins once each day. In fact, these satellites orbit once each day, too. They seem to stay over the same spot on the surface, all the time.

This is called a geostationary orbit. It makes signalling to the satellite much easier. The ground stations do not have to track the satellite across the sky, because it just 'hangs' in the same place, all day and all night.

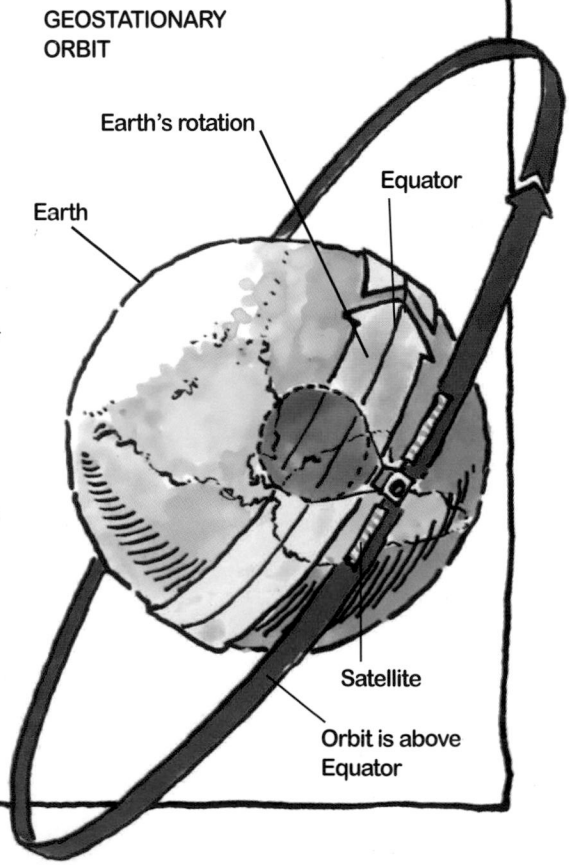

THE MAP

A map gives a bird's eye view of an area – from a few fields or streets, to the whole world. The golden age of map-making and exploration was about 1400-1800. If Christopher Columbus, Ferdinand Magellan and James Cook had not sailed the oceans and mapped the world, we might still think it was flat!

One of the first maps, carved on a piece of bone, shows a tiny area now called Mezhirich, Russia. It is 12,000 years old.

The Ancient Greeks and Romans were the first good map-makers. They sailed the Mediterranean and mapped its coastline. Their soldiers explored and conquered new lands. So they had good maps of Europe, North Africa and the Middle East – but not much else.

Mappa Mundi

Mappa Mundi

In the Middle Ages, a well-known map called the Mappa Mundi showed Jerusalem in the centre of a flat Earth. Asia was at the top, Europe at the lower left, and Africa lower right.

In 1519-1522, Magellan's expedition sailed around the world and showed that the Earth was ball-shaped.

Since that time, hundreds of map-making expeditions have studied all parts of the land and the sea bed.

Ferdinand Magellan

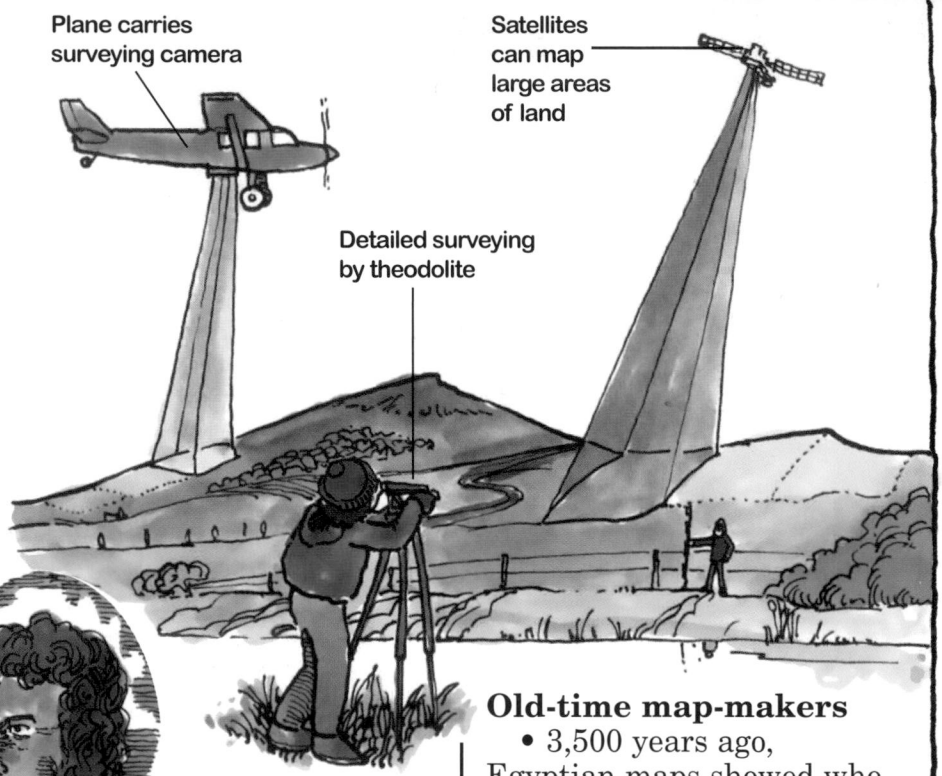

Changing maps

Today, aeroplanes and satellites with survey cameras make ever more detailed maps. They show mountains and valleys, soil and rock types, croplands and cities. They are used by almost everyone, from road planners to tourists.

Maps change. Wars alter national borders. Dams make new lakes. There are new roads, bridges and tunnels. Look at an old map, and see. Maps changed the world – and the world changes maps!

Old-time map-makers

• 3,500 years ago, Egyptian maps showed who owned the lowlands along the River Nile. This is because when the river flooded each year, it washed away boundary fences and marker posts.

• People once believed if you sailed off the edge of the flat Earth, you fell into the fire belching from the mouth of a giant dragon.

THE CAMERA

'Smile, please. Watch the birdie. Say cheese. Go back a bit more – Oh, I didn't see that cliff!' Cameras take holiday snaps, photos for newspapers, books and magazines, home videos, and movies for the big screen.

The first camera was the camera obscura ('dark chamber'), a room or box with a small hole in one side. Light shone through the hole and was reflected down to make a light picture on a screen.

Camera obscura

Astronomers watched eclipses with them, and artists traced landscapes from them. During the 1600s, the hole was filled by a glass lens, to make the image clearer and brighter.

Capturing the image

From the 1800s, people tried to record the light image. They shone it onto a plate of chemicals. The light changed the chemicals, making a visible picture.

In 1826, Nicéphore Niépce produced the first permanent photograph, on chemical-coated pewter metal. In 1839, Louis Daguerre announced a better method using 'wet' metal plates. However, each photograph was still a one-off.

In the same year, Henry Talbot's chemical-coated paper recorded the image as a negative, with light areas dark, and dark areas light. But it had an advantage. With more chemicals and paper, many positives – known as 'prints' – could be made from one negative.

What a good idea!

George Eastman, head of Kodak, brought photography to ordinary people. In 1888, Kodak produced a camera loaded with film for 100 pictures. You took the snaps and sent the whole camera back for processing and reloading. Next came the Kodak Brownie #1.

Digi-cameras

By the early 1990s, movie and stills cameras were recording light using a chip called a CCD, or charge-coupled device. This records light as tiny electrical signals, which are stored in electronic memory cards or sticks, and sent over the Internet. Then laptops, cellphones and other small gadgets got cameras too. Never has it been easier to bore your friends with your holiday photos.

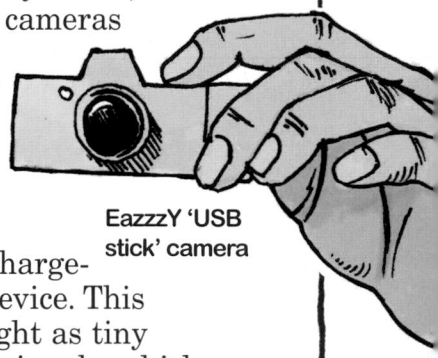

EazzzY 'USB stick' camera

Nicéphore Niépce

EARLY CAMERA

Plate holder

Lightproof box

Aperture ring

Focusing control

Sensitive glass plate

Lens

Lens cap removed for exposure

OIL

Drill into the ground, find 'Black Gold',
Thick and sticky and not very cold.
Pump it out and get it sold,
By tanker and pipeline, to refinery,
Where the huge petroleum industry,
Oils the wheels of machinery.
Making plastics, asphalts, tars and wax,
Fuels for cars and trucks, jets and stacks...
of other stuff!

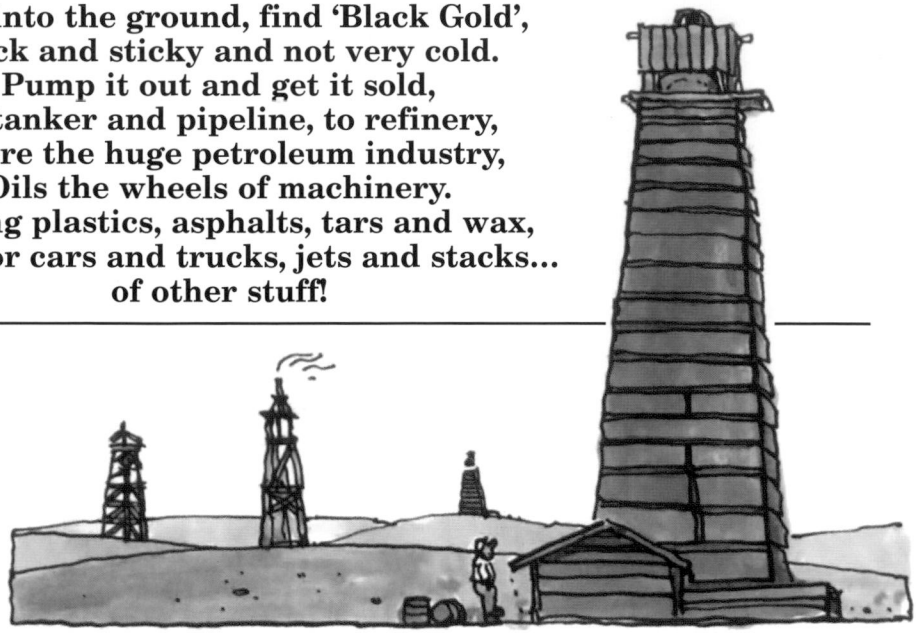

Oil is so important in the modern world that nations threaten each other with oil bans, and fight wars over oilfields.

Millions of people are employed in the oil business, or petroleum industry. They search for it, drill it out, and transport it to huge chemical refineries. Here its ingredients are separated and made into a multitude of raw materials.

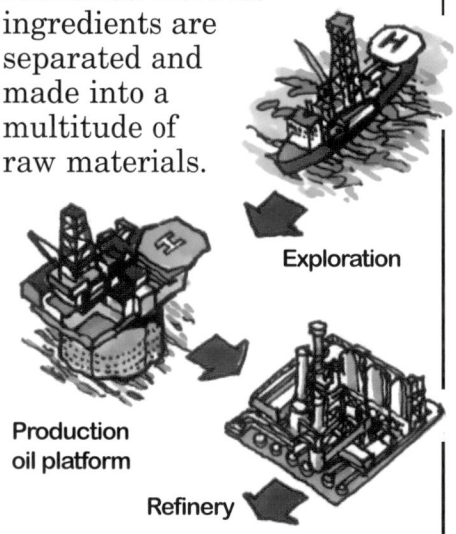

A grinding halt

Without oil, the modern world would truly grind to a halt. Machines would have no lubricating oils, so they would seize up. Vehicles and planes would have no fuel. Millions of people who burn heating oil would get cold.

We'd have fewer plastics for electrical products, toys, plumbing and a host of other uses. There'd be no asphalt on roads, and no artificial fibres like nylon. There'd be far fewer farm and factory chemicals, glues, paints, detergents and soaps. No plastic bags, fewer carpets, medicines, artificial blood vessels ...

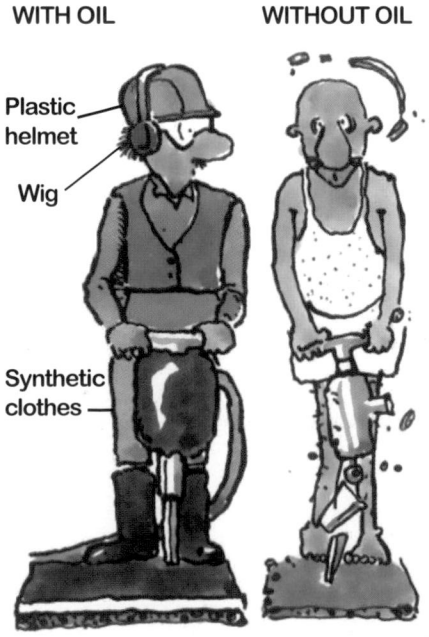

The first oil wells

People used oils for thousands of years, for lamps, cooking, heating and lubrication. The oils often came from animals, such as sheep or great whales. Or they were scooped from natural oil and tar pits on the ground.

In 1859 at Titusville, in Pennsylvania, USA, Colonel Edwin Drake and his crew drilled a hole into the ground. It took about two months. On 27 August the oil began to flow, marking the start of the petroleum industry.

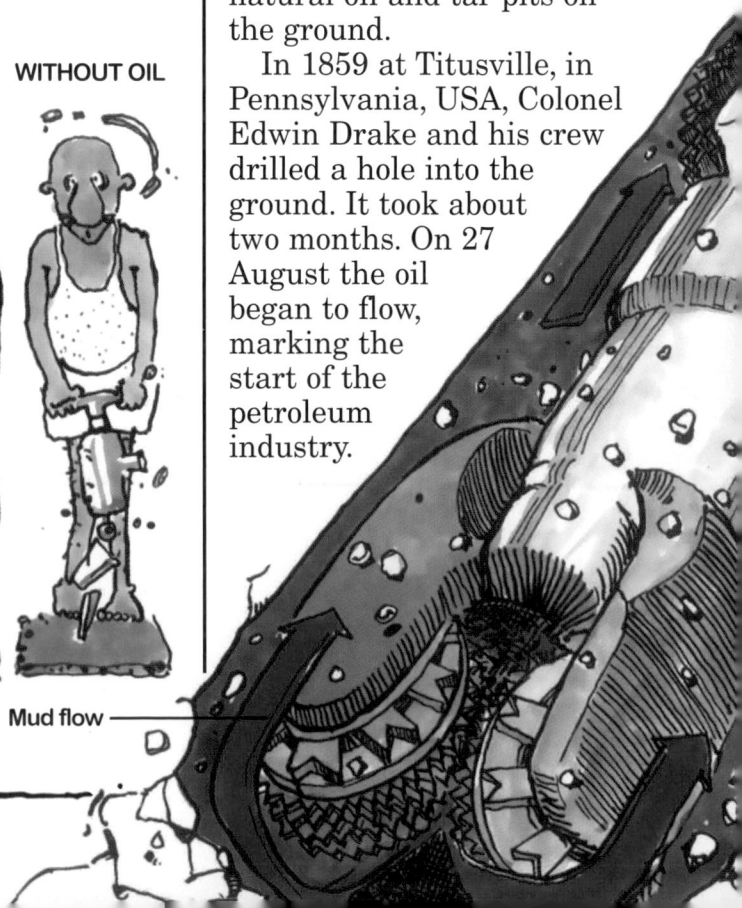

Derrick

Drill sections

Safety valve

Concrete lining

Secondary drill bit

Impervious rock stops oil filtering to the surface

Trapped oil

Drilling

Oil is a liquid fossil. Millions of years ago it was tiny plants and animals, floating in the sea. They died, got buried, formed rocks, and slowly changed to oil and natural gas.

Drilling a hole to find oil is expensive. So scientists do many surveys and tests, such as making a mini-earthquake with explosives, to check oil is there.

Then a huge tower called Derek – sorry, a derrick – is built for the drill. The derrick is on the land above the oil, or on a platform if the oil is under the sea bed. The drill has a diamond-studded bit and screw-together sections 9 metres long. The final hole may be 10,000 metres deep! When it reaches a pool of oil, the oil may ooze to the surface under its own pressure. Or it's forced up by pumping water or mud down the outer ring of the well hole.

Refining

The thick, dark stuff that comes out of the well is called crude oil or petroleum. It is taken by pipeline or oil tanker to the refinery. This is a giant chemical factory where oil is split into its components.

The crude oil flows into a tall tower called the fractionation column. This is hottest at the base, and cooler near the top. The various parts, or fractions, of the crude boil off as vapours. They cool and condense at their own level in the tower, and flow away along pipes for more purifying.

Nasty gushers

• When oil spurts out of control from a well, it's called a wildcat. In 1956 in Qum, Iran, oil gushed 50 metres high. In 2010 the Deepwater Horizon rig in the Gulf of Mexico suffered a massive underwater blowout, killing 11 people and polluting vast areas.

FRACTIONATION OR DISTILLATION COLUMN

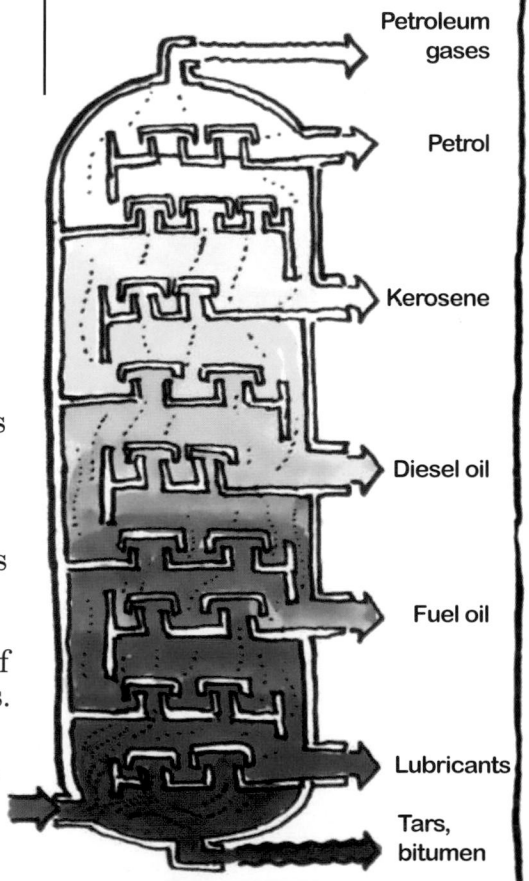

ELECTRONICS, COMPUTERS & THE INTERNET

Microchips aren't what you eat with a very small burger. They are hundreds and thousands of electronic components on wafers of silicon smaller than your fingernail. They are the basis of our electronic digital world, all kinds of computers, and the all-knowing Internet.

It's the Electronic Age. Microchips and other tiny electronic devices affect almost everything we do, from switching TV channels to making a phone call. Our gadget-mad world is electronically controlled. And the speed of change is breathtaking.

Faster and cheaper

Fifty years ago, computers took up whole rooms. They needed air-conditioning, and enough electricity for a whole factory. One of the first electronic chip devices to make it onto the mass market was the humble pocket calculator, in the 1970s. Now almost every small electronic gadget, even a camera or smartphone, has a built-in calculator function.

Pocket calculator

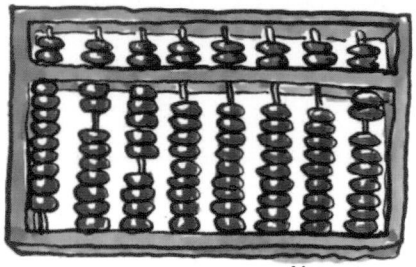

Abacus

Beads to valves

The abacus, invented around AD 300, is still used in Eastern Asia. It's a memory aid for the user's mental sums. The column of beads on the right represents 1s, the next one is 10s, then 100s, and so on.

Colossus was an early computer which could be programmed. It lived in Buckinghamshire in 1943, helping to break codes in World War Two.

A famous early computer was Eniac, at the University of Pennsylvania, USA, in 1946. It could do 300 sums each second, but connections had to be changed for each new type of calculation.

Valves to transistors

Valves were early electronic devices. They could switch, strengthen, reverse and alter tiny electrical signals. But they were as big as light bulbs, got hot, used lots of electricity, and tended to burn out.

Valve

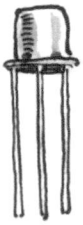

Transistors arrived in the late 1940s. They did similar jobs to valves, but they were much smaller, more efficient, and faster. By the 1960s, battery-powered portable transistor radios were all the rage.

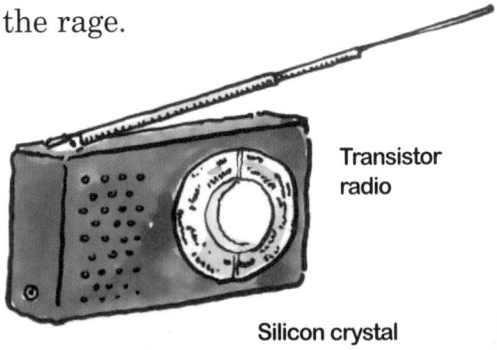

Transistor radio

Silicon crystal

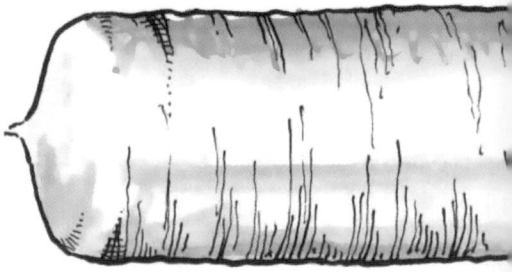

The coming of the chips

The first microchips appeared in the 1960s. They combined or integrated loads of components, such as transistors, diodes, resistors, and capacitors, into one circuit, on a chip of silicon – the 'integrated circuit'. It was a great advance.

Silicon is not a really good conductor of electricity, or a very bad one. It's a semiconductor. Wires, contacts and components can be made by etching patterns into a wafer of it, by processes using light or X-rays.

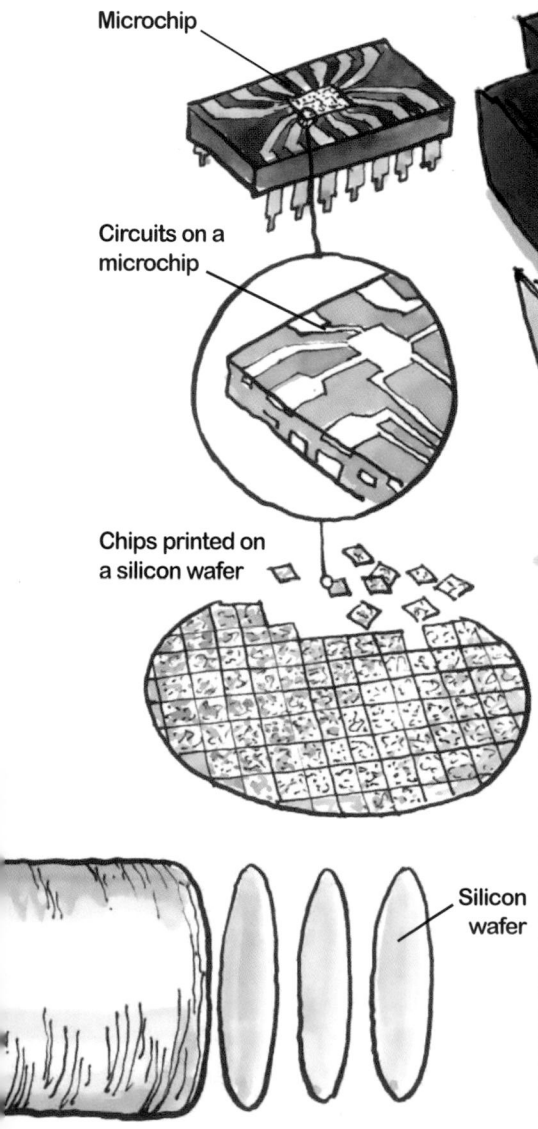

Chips everywhere

Today, microchips control the electrical workings of hundreds of devices. They save petrol in cars by adjusting the engine, turn your TV recorder on when you're out, and recognise magnetic codes in credit cards and bar codes in supermarkets. And they are vital to computers, which affect all modern life.

The Internet

In the late 1950s, the US Military had the idea of linking their computers by wires, even those in different cities, so they could all work together faster.

From this simple beginning came the impossibly complicated international, integrated, interconnected network of computers and other gadgets we have today – the Internet. In 1989 British scientist Tim Berners-Lee had the idea for sharing documents, then pictures, music and other items, over the Internet. This quickly became the WorldWide Web, as in www (dot). The Net and Web do not so much change our lives, as control them.

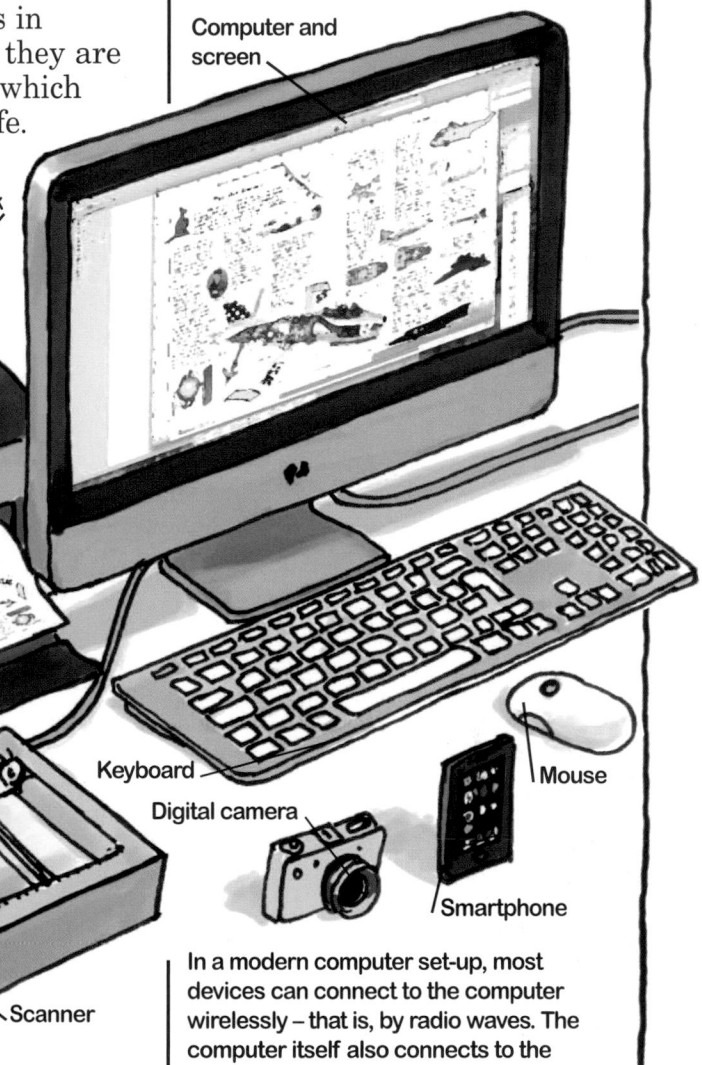

In a modern computer set-up, most devices can connect to the computer wirelessly – that is, by radio waves. The computer itself also connects to the Internet wirelessly. The only wires needed are to bring electrical power.

THE ATOMIC BOMB

In a split second in 1945, the world changed forever. In the Pacific, World War Two was dragging on. At 7:30 am on 6 August, the Allies dropped the first atomic bomb over the Japanese city of Hiroshima. The death and destruction was immense. In a few days, war ended. The shadow of atomic and nuclear weapons has been with us ever since.

'Little Boy' was a metal-cased bomb about 2 metres long. Exploding over Hiroshima, it killed some 75,000 people and flattened three-fifths of the city. Thousands more died later from injuries, burns and radiation sickness.

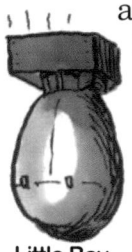

Little Boy

How the bomb worked

'Little Boy' had gigantic destructive power because it turned matter into energy. The matter was in the form of the radioactive substance uranium-235.

At the critical moment, two pieces of uranium-235 crashed together in the bomb. Some of the uranium atoms split, in a process called nuclear fission. The resulting atomic fragments weighed less than the original atoms, because parts of them were converted to energy – in the form of light, heat and radioactivity. The fission also made more fast-moving atomic fragments, which collided with other uranium atoms, splitting them too, and so on, in a split-second chain reaction.

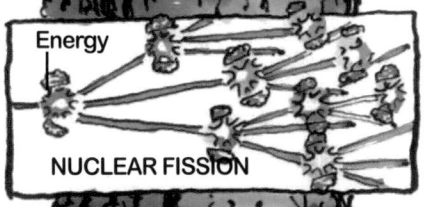

Nuclear weapons today

After the war, enough atomic bombs were made to blast the whole world to pieces many times.

Then came hydrogen bombs, which were even more powerful. Their energy was released when atomic bits of hydrogen joined together, in atomic fusion. Different types of hydrogen bombs form the bulk of today's nuclear weapons.

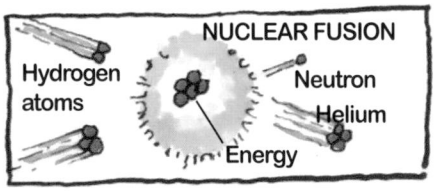

Power to destroy

- One of the most powerful chemical high-explosives is TNT.
- An atomic bomb, or A-bomb, is a million times more powerful than a TNT bomb of the same size.
- A hydrogen bomb or H-bomb is a thousand times more powerful than an A-bomb of the same size.

FUSION POWER – *HALF AN INVENTION?*

A safe, cheap, reliable source of energy, that won't pollute the world or run out. Sounds like a dream? It has been. But scientists are trying to make the dream real. Fusion power could not only change the world, but save it, too.

The hydrogen bombs described opposite work by nuclear fusion. But their energy is released all at once, in a massive BANG. Could the process be controlled in a fusion reactor? Experiments in the past few years show – hopefully, yes.

A TYPICAL NUCLEAR FISSION POWER STATION

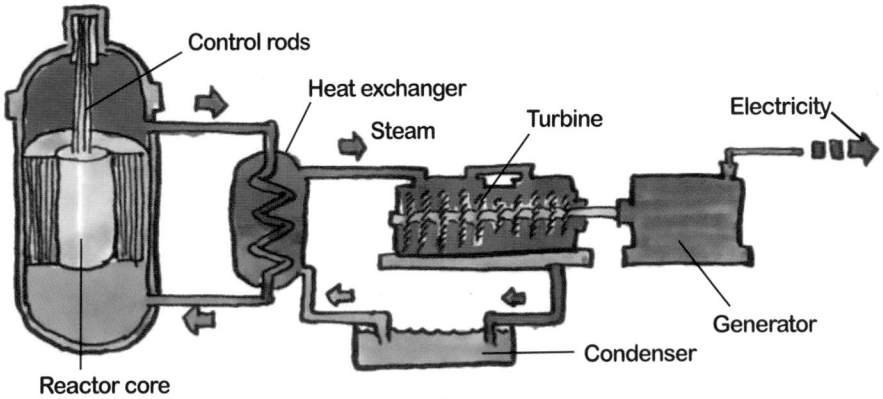

Plasma-filled donut

A fusion reactor would be shaped like a donut, and called a torus. Inside, two forms of hydrogen called deuterium and tritium must be heated to an incredible 100 million°C, as they whirl around. At this temperature they are not solid, liquid or gas. They are another form of matter, plasma.

Some of the atomic bits in the plasma of deuterium and tritium join together, or fuse. They produce atomic bits of another substance, helium, and also give out vast amounts of heat and other energy. The heat could power electricity generators, as in a normal power station.

Copying the Sun

Today's nuclear power stations use fission reactors which split atoms, like the atomic bomb (opposite). In theory, fusion power could be cleaner, less dangerous and less polluting. But it will take many years and experiments before fusion power changes the world.

Even so, we already rely on it! Bits of hydrogen atoms fuse to form helium, creating light and heat and other energy – in the Sun.

TOKAMAK experimental fusion reactor

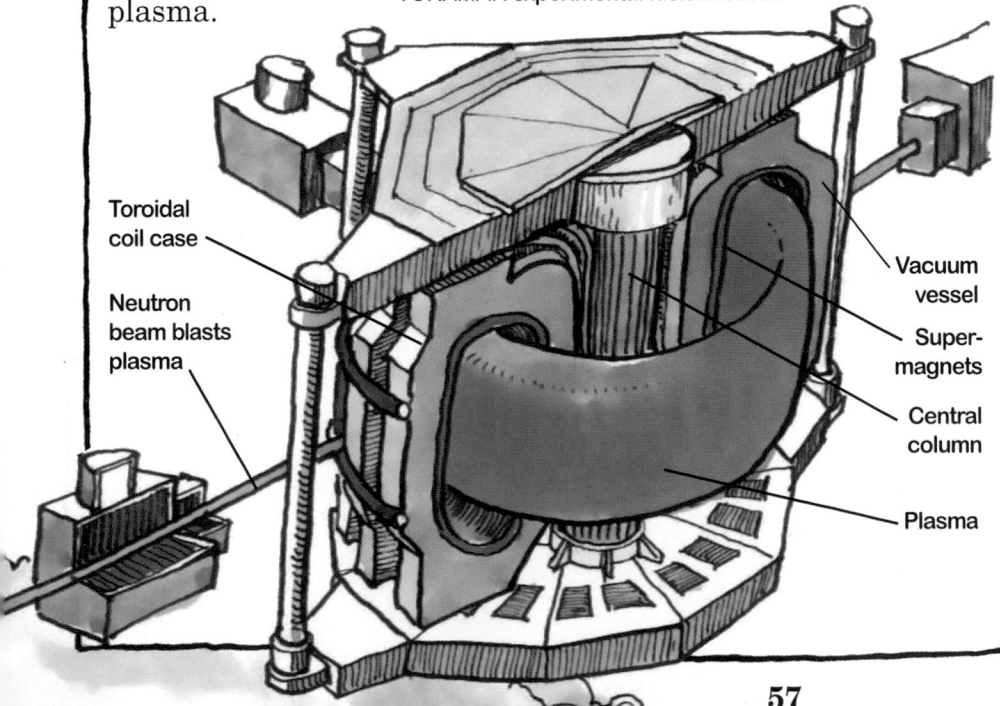

Cold fusion fails

• In the early 1990s there was a great argument about 'cold fusion', where fusion power might be made at ordinary temperatures. A few scientists claimed they got it to work. Others repeated the experiments, but they didn't work. No one has proved 'cold fusion' since.

... AND THINGS THAT DIDN'T

The bottom line is that humans can exist on just food, water and a bit of shelter. Things like cars, cellphones, printing and music are not truly vital to life – even though, as we've seen, they have changed the world.

For every invention and advance that has altered the way we live, hundreds of others haven't. These inventions may be interesting or boring, serious or amusing, useful or downright useless. But they have not deeply affected daily life. Most of us could do without them. Could you?

The safety pin

This metal gadget was being used in Ancient Egypt over 4,500 years ago. It was 'safe' because the sharp end of the pin slipped into a cover. Some designs looked like coiled serpents.

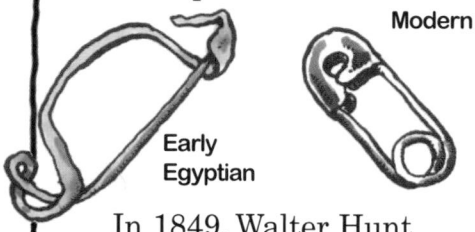

In 1849, Walter Hunt reinvented the safety pin. When a button or zip breaks, look for one. But how often do you find it? Oh well, back to the needle and thread.

The rattle

Toys are as old – or young – as babies and children. It's said that 2,400 years ago in Ancient Greece, the philosopher Archytas, a friend of Plato, invented the baby's rattle. He gave rattles to the families of slaves. He said that if children could make a noise, they would not break and wreck things.

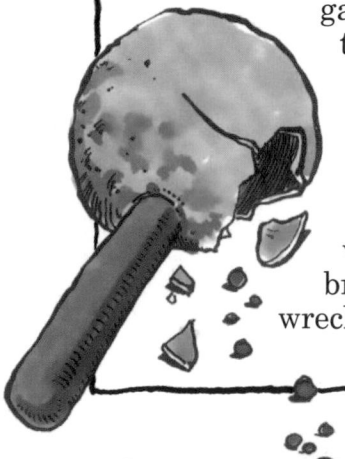

Tame cats

You might argue that cats aren't tame. They only use us for food and warmth. Cats were loved and worshipped in Ancient Egypt. In the Middle Ages lots of families in Europe kept cats, to kill rats, which carried fleas, which spread the Plague. Yet around the world, many other creatures live with people and keep down pests. They include mongooses, martens, dogs, jackals, falcons, even snakes and lions.

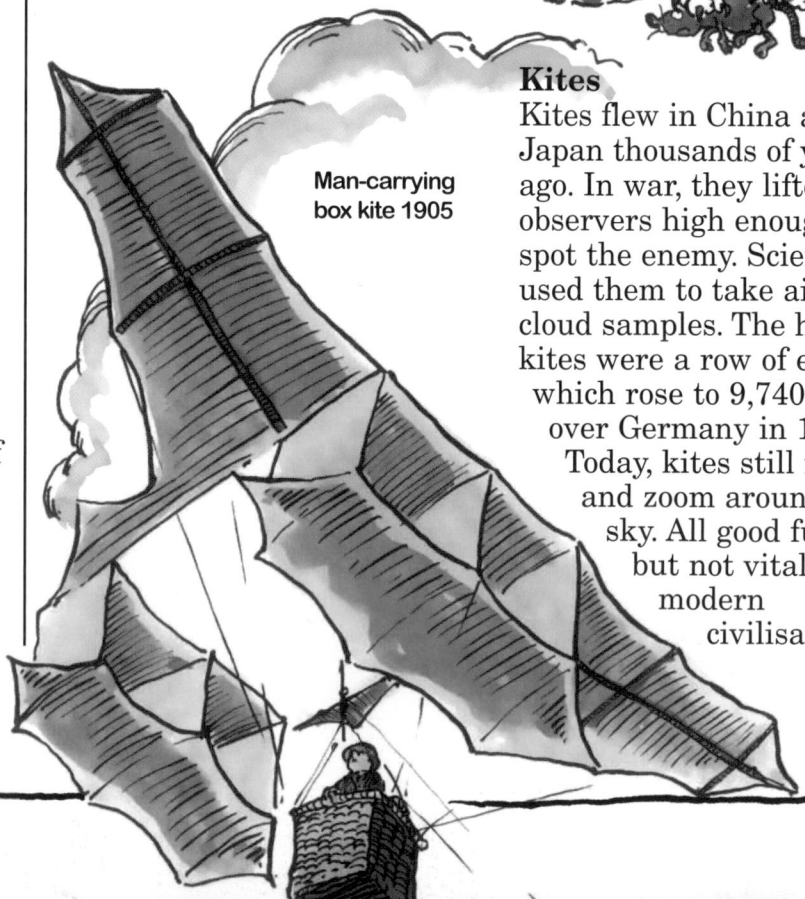

Kites

Kites flew in China and Japan thousands of years ago. In war, they lifted observers high enough to spot the enemy. Scientists used them to take air and cloud samples. The highest kites were a row of eight, which rose to 9,740 metres over Germany in 1919. Today, kites still flap and zoom around the sky. All good fun, but not vital to modern civilisation.

Napkins
In olden times, people didn't bother to wipe their mouths or hands after eating a messy meal. As they became more aware of cleanliness they used tablecloths, and wiped their mouths on these. In the late 15th Century, napkins appeared for cleaning knives, forks, mouths and fingers.

Chess
Chess, the champion board game, may have come from a game called chaturanga, played in India about 1,200 years ago. The chess pieces we know today appeared in Europe in the 15th Century. The first proper chess book was published by French musician Francois Philidor in 1749. Millions of people play and enjoy chess, but life would go on without it.

National anthems
In modern times, the first country to adopt a song as its own tune was Switzerland, in about 1600. Britain's *God Save the Queen* (or *King*) was written in 1740. France's *Marseillaise* of 1792 celebrated the French Revolution. There's still a good trade in national anthems, as countries fight and split and join and set up new states.

The umbrella
Ancient peoples used non-folding umbrellas against rain and sun. The modern version with folding metal spokes was developed in England in the 17th century, mainly as a parasol or sunshade. If you had an umbrella with silk panels, and a shaft of beautifully carved ivory, you were very rich.

The sandwich
In the mid-1700s, the Earl of Sandwich was so keen on gambling that he didn't want to stop for meals. Servants brought his meals of meat, placed between pieces of bread, so they were easy to carry. A snack was born. Lucky he wasn't the Earl of Yuksnotbag.

The rocking chair
American scientist and statesman Benjamin Franklin is credited with many ideas and inventions. A story says that in the 1750s, he noticed how a baby rocked in a cradle soon went to sleep. So he put cradle rockers on an ordinary chair, for grown-ups to rock themselves to snoozeland.

Aaaah, restful, but beware squashing your toes! Remember the old saying: 'He's as nervous as a long-tailed cat in a roomful of rocking chairs.'

Invisible ink
What's the use of ink you can't see? You make it visible by treating it in some way. Not by taking it to a movie, but by heating it or painting it with a special chemical.

An early invisible ink consisted of a mixture of milk and lemon juice, and was used in England, in the 1770s. Write and let it dry – nothing. But with gentle warmth, it turned brown. It was used by people to send secret messages.

Chewing gum
Thomas Adams, an American inventor, developed chewing gum in the 1870s. It was based on a natural rubbery substance called chicle, which oozes from the sapodilla tree of Central America. The Mayan people of Mexico chomped on chicle, a thousand years ago. Its chewability was rediscovered in the search for better rubbery substances for industry. Can you think of a flavour you can't buy?

Cornflakes
In the 1890s, the Kelloggs lived in Battle Creek, Michigan, USA. They were a large family – about 15 children. Will Kellogg, with his brother John, invented a method of toasting flakes of corn, to make a healthy yet cheap snack. In 1906 Will masterminded the Battle Creek Toasted Corn Flakes Competition. His company, Kelloggs, the maker of breakfast cereals, is still going strong.

Horse-racing on stage
In 1890 the Union Square Theatre in New York, USA, staged real horse races. Jockeys rode their mounts on a huge conveyor-like treadmill built into the stage. A man controlled the electric motors which moved the treadmill and the scenery behind.

The teddy bear
This cuddly toy became famous in 1903. It was named after Theodore 'Teddy' Roosevelt, the US President, who saved a real bear cub on a hunting trip. Toy-makers soon saw their chance to sell furry bears and make lots of money.

Electric-arc iron
Smoothing irons were warmed over a fire or had a lump of hot metal inside. When electricity was first available in homes, around 1900, early electric irons had a carbon arc inside. Electricity jumped as a huge spark across the gap between two rods of carbon. It made an intense light, a crackling noise, and heat. Luckily, it was soon followed by the heater-element iron we (well, some of us) use today.

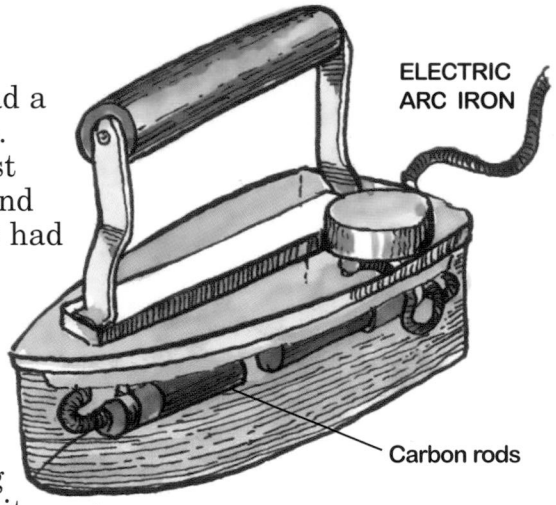

Spruce Goose
This vast aeroplane was built in the 1940s by movie multi-millionaire Howard Hughes. It was a flying boat made of wood, with eight propellers and a wingspan of 97.5 metres (a Jumbo Jet's is 60 metres). It was supposed to carry loads of soldiers and supplies from the USA to Europe, to win World War Two. But it flew only once, for 1,500 metres in 1947. It's now in Evergreen Aviation Museum near Portland, Oregon.

The Mackerel car
In the 1960s a Swedish inventor came up with a car that had numerous sausage-shaped balloons around each wheel. An air pump and valves controlled their inflation and deflation. On each wheel they blew up the sausage just behind the one flat on the ground, and let down the sausage in front.

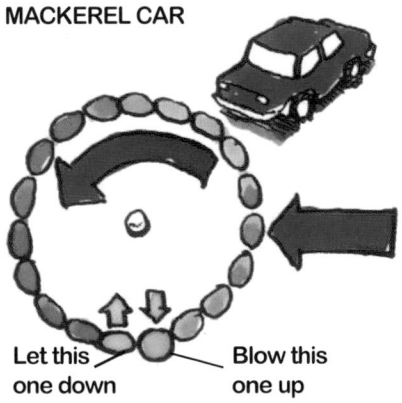

Do this fast, and hey presto, the wheel rolls forwards! No one took up the idea.

The mini-skirt
Skirt hemlines have gone up and down through the ages. In the early 1960s, fashion designer Mary Quant unveiled the miniskirt. It was very short and used less material, yet it often cost more than a long skirt! Some people said it was fun, others said it was daring or disgraceful. Miniskirts have come in and out of fashion since.

And finally ... electric transport?
There have been several tries at electric cars and bikes. The electric bike is easy to ride, and low-polluting. But it's very difficult to get people out of their cars – which can be hybrid, fuel-cell, or battery.

Will electric bikes and hydrogen fuel-cell cars alter our lives? Maybe. Guessing the next invention that will change the world is all part of the fun.

INDEX

A
abacus 54
aeroplane 21, 39, 42, 43, 44-45, 61
anaesthetics 26
anthracite 14
antibiotics 26
antiseptics 26
arc lamps 28
Archimedean screw 21
armies 10
art 7, 8
atomic bombs 56, 57

B
batteries 29, 61
Bell, Alexander Graham 34, 35
bikes 61
blast furnace 14
boats and ships 10, 20, 21, 39
books 24, 25
bronze 9
buildings 8

C
cameras 51
carpentry 21
cars 39, 41, 45, 61
cassettes 31
cats 58
cave paintings 7
CCDs 51
cellphones (mobiles) 31, 34-35, 36, 51, 54
cells 23
chess 59
chewing gum 60
chronometers 16
cities and towns 8
clippers 20
clocks 16
clothes 7, 61
coke 14
combine harvesters 19
communications satellites 48, 49
compact discs 31
computers 54, 55
cornflakes 60

D
democratic governments 11
diesel engines 40, 41
diseases 23, 27
doctors 26
domestic animals 8, 9, 58

E
early man 6-7
Edison, Thomas 28, 30
electric cars 29, 41, 61
electric irons 61
electric motors 29
electricity 28-29, 34, 36, 37, 39, 61
electron microscopes 23
electronics 54-55
endoscopes 27
explosives 32, 33, 56

F
farming 8, 10, 18-19
fashion 61
film industry 51
fire 6
fusion power 57

G
Galileo 22
glass 11
gliders 42
gods and spirits 8
gramophones 30, 31
Great Plague 27, 58
gunpowder 32, 33, 41
guns 32-33
Gutenberg Bible 24
Guy Fawkes 33

H
harpsichords 17
helicopter 45
horses 9, 60
hot-air balloons 42
hybrid cars 41, 61
hydrogen bomb 56-57
hydrogen fuel cell 61

I
internal combustion engines 40-41
Internet 35, 48, 51, 54-55
invisible ink 60
iPod 31, 55
iron 9, 14

J
jet engines 44-45

K
kites 58

L
laws 11
light bulbs 28
Linotype machines 25
lithography 25
locomotives 39

M
malaria 27
maps 50
matchlocks 32
medicine 23, 26-27
metals 9, 14
microbiology 23
microchips 54, 55
microscopes 22, 23
miniskirts 61
mobile phones (cellphones) 31, 34-35, 36, 51, 54
Moon landings 29, 46
Morse code 34, 36
mp3 players 31
music 7, 8, 17, 31
musical instruments 7, 17

N
napkins 59
national anthems 59
navigation 16
nuclear power 57
nuclear weapons 56
nuts and bolts 21

O
oil 52-53

P
pain relief 26
penicillin 26
petrol engines 40, 41, 43
petroleum 53
phonographs 30
photography 51
pianos 17
ploughs 18
pottery 9, 10
printing 24-25
propellers 21, 42, 44, 45

R
radio-telescopes 23
radios 36, 54
railways 39
rattles 58
record discs 31
religion 8
revolvers 33
rifles 33
roads 15
rocking chairs 59
rulers 11

S
safety pins 58
sailing ships 20
sandwiches 59
satellites 47, 48-49
scanners 27
schools 11
screw-propellers 21
screws 21
silicon 55
Sinclair C5 29
space research 47
space rocket 46-47
space shuttle 46, 47, 49
spy satellites 49
steam engines 38-39, 43
steel 14
surgery 26

T
tape recorders 31
tarmac 15
teddy bears 60
telephones 34-35
telescopes 22, 23
televisions 37
threshing machines 19
time-keeping 16
toilets 12-13
tools 6, 9
tractors 18, 19, 39
transistors 54, 55

U
umbrellas 59

V
valves 54
video camera 51
vinyl records 30-31

W
warfare 10, 32, 43, 44-45, 46, 56
weapons 9, 32-33, 56
wheels 9, 15
wines and beers 9
wristwatch 16

X
X-rays 27, 49, 55

First published MCMXCII by Simon & Schuster Young Books
Revised and updated edition published by Book House MMXII